MEDITATIONS
for MOTHERS

12 Reflections on THE BETTER PART
A CHRIST-CENTERED RESOURCE *for* PERSONAL PRAYER

JOHN BARTUNEK, LC

CIRCLE
PRESS

Cover and interior design by Lisa Fiducia

Cover image copyright © Getty Images
Interior floral images copyright © iStock.com The following images
copyright © Art Resource, NY: p.8 Finsiel/Alinari; p.15 Tate London;
p.16 Bildarchiv Preussischer Kulturbesitz; p.26 Fine Art Photographic
Library, London; p.59 HIP; p.62 The Philadelphia Museum of Art;
p.72 Scala; p.88 HP. Images on pp. 36, 52, 80, 107 copyright © www.
ArchivalArt.com. *Maternal Kiss*, Mary Cassatt p.44 & *On the Terrace*,
Pierre-Auguste Renoir, Wikipedia Art; "Uncle Eddy" emails pp 32, 104
used with permission of www.catholic.net.

Gospel text taken from *The Jerusalem Bible* by Alexander Jones, ed.,
copyright © 1966 by Dartman, Longman & Todd, LTD, and Doubleday,
a division of Random House, Inc. Used by permission of Doubleday, a
division of Random House, Inc.

Imprimi Potest:
Francisco Mateos, LC

Nihil Obstat
Imprimatur
† Most Reverend Henry J. Mansell
Archbishop of Hartford
June 14, 2007

CIP data is on file with the Library of Congress
ISBN 978-1-933271-26-2

PRINTED IN THE UNITED STATES OF AMERICA

8 7 6 5 4 3 2 1

FIRST EDITION

Table of Contents

Introduction

The last thing I saw on my mother's face before she died was her smile. I was only nine years old, but I can still picture it perfectly. We had watched multiple sclerosis take her from cane to walker to wheelchair – and now she was bedridden, in a nursing home. It was the last time my two sisters and I would see her. And when I told her that I had just, for the first time, joined a little league basketball team, her eyes lit up, and she smiled. Ever since then, whenever I think of her I see that smile, and it makes *me* smile – even, sometimes, through my tears.

Isn't a mother's smile the first thing every baby sees? Isn't a mother's smile the key that heals a child's every hurt, opens the slammed doors of anger and discouragement, and unlocks the hidden treasures of a youthful heart? All of us are children, and all of us can testify to the magic of our mother's smile (and the menace of her frown!). But only some of you are mothers. This little book is for you.

The fallen world in which you struggle to work your mother's magic is not kind to motherhood. The devil's first sortie against the human race was directed at the world's first mother – and his tactics haven't changed. Legalized abortion, the exploitation and objectification of women in the media, rampant divorce, the normalization of homosexuality... These are modern variations on his ancient theme, new efforts to banish mothers' smiles. They cannot succeed completely, but they do their damage, and even well-intentioned, wise, and faithful mothers feel their effect.

Yet the devil is no match for Jesus. To redeem the human race, his first move was to redeem motherhood. To raise the fallen world, his first step was to give us a new Eve: Mary, full of grace, true Mother of the Redeemer, and true spiritual mother for us, who have become Jesus' brothers and sisters through grace and faith.

God invented motherhood, and Jesus redeemed it. And so there is no better place to find inspiration, strength, and comfort as you strive to fulfill your motherly mission than in his Word. This volume brings together Gospel passages, commentaries from *The Better Part: A Christ-Centered Resource for Personal Prayer,* and other jewels from our spiritual and cultural heritage, all of which have been chosen with that goal in mind.

Keep it nearby, dip into it, mark it up, or read it straight through. However you choose to use it, you are sure to find here something that will remind you of the greatness and beauty of your calling. May those reminders never fail to refresh your mother's smile and thereby help bring to everyone around you the inspiration that only you, as a mother, can bring.

Thanks!

Thank you, ***women who are mothers!*** You have sheltered human beings within yourselves in a unique experience of joy and travail. This experience makes you become God's own smile upon the newborn child, the one who guides your child's first steps, who helps it to grow, and who is the anchor as the child makes its way along the journey of life.

Thank you, ***women who are wives!*** You irrevocably join your future to that of your husbands, in a relationship of mutual giving, at the service of love and life.

Thank you, ***women who are daughters*** and ***women who are sisters!*** Into the heart of the family, and then of all society, you bring the richness of your sensitivity, your intuitiveness, your generosity and fidelity.

Thank you, ***women who work!*** You are present and active in every area of life – social, economic, cultural, artistic and political. In this way you make an indispensable contribution to the growth of a culture which unites reason and feeling, to a model of life ever open to the sense of "mystery," to the establishment of economic and political structures ever more worthy of humanity.

Thank you, ***consecrated women!*** Following the example of the greatest of women, the Mother of Jesus Christ, the Incarnate Word, you open yourselves with obedience and fidelity to the gift of God's love. You help the Church and all mankind to experience a "spousal" relationship to God, one which magnificently expresses the fellowship which God wishes to establish with his creatures.

Meditations for Mothers

Thank you, ***every woman,*** for the simple fact of being a woman! Through the insight which is so much a part of your womanhood you enrich the world's understanding and help to make human relations more honest and authentic.

- POPE JOHN PAUL II, *LETTER TO WOMEN,* JUNE 29, 1995

The level of any society is the level of its womanhood.

ARCHBISHOP FULTON J. SHEEN

The Greatest Yes

"Therefore, though it is God who takes
the initiative of coming to dwell in the
midst of men, and he is always the main
architect of this plan, it is also true that
he does not will to carry it out without
our active cooperation."

POPE BENEDICT XVI

LUKE 1:26-38

In the sixth month the angel Gabriel was sent by God to a town in Galilee called Nazareth, to a virgin betrothed to a man named Joseph, of the House of David; and the virgin's name was Mary. He went in and said to her, 'Rejoice, so highly favoured! The Lord is with you.' She was deeply disturbed by these words and asked herself what this greeting could mean, but the angel said to her, 'Mary, do not be afraid; you have won God's favour. Listen! You are to conceive and bear a son, and you must name him Jesus. He will be great and will be called Son of the Most High. The Lord God will give him the throne of his ancestor David; he will rule over the House of Jacob for ever and his reign will have no end.' Mary said to the angel, 'But how can this come about, since I am a virgin?' 'The Holy Spirit will come upon you,' the angel answered, 'and the power of the Most High will cover you with its shadow. And so the child will be holy and will be called Son of God. Know this too: your kinswoman Elizabeth has, in her old age, herself conceived a son, and she whom people called barren is now in her sixth month, for nothing is impossible to God.' 'I am the handmaid of the Lord,' said Mary; 'let what you have said be done to me.' And the angel left her.

CHRIST THE LORD ⁓

Of whom can it be said, "His reign will have no end"? Only of Jesus Christ, the Son of God and the son of David (from whose descendents the promised Messiah was to be born), and the only man ever born of a virgin. Gabriel's brief announcement to Mary foretells the advent of someone absolutely unique: the Davidic king who will rule over all the nations, the one who would save mankind from their sins ("Jesus" means "God saves"), and the one who would fulfill all the Old Testament prophecies about the reunification of Israel and Judah (the "House of Jacob"). The entire Gospel is packed into this Annunciation of the Archangel Gabriel to Mary.

It is a Gospel that at times is hard to believe. Sometimes it seems almost too good to be true – too simple, too easy. On the other hand, when the sufferings and tragedies of life and the tumultuous twists and turns of human history oppress us, it seems more like a fairy tale, a pipe dream. For Mary too the announcement was almost overwhelming. But her faith and purity sensitized her to God's truth. She accepted the angel's message and all its implications for her own life – a radical, unforeseen change in her plans. She was able to do so because she had long ago assimilated a doctrine we too often ignore, one that Gabriel reminded her of: "Nothing is impossible for God."

CHRIST THE TEACHER ⁓

Christmas, the part of Christ's life this Gospel passage is connected to, presents us with the mystery of God who became man, but it also includes the mystery of man cooperating in the saving action of God. God sends his messenger to Mary in order to invite her to become the mother of the Savior. She accepted the invitation, and history has never been the same. But it would have been possible for her to reject it. Like the parable Christ tells of the many townspeople who decline the king's invitation to attend his son's wedding feast, Mary could have considered God's intervention just a disruption of her plans, an inconvenience. But she did not.

When God asked her to take on a role in his plan of salvation, she said yes: "I am the handmaid of the Lord, let what you have said be done to me." Her question to the archangel, "But how can this come about, since I am a virgin?" was different than the similar sounding question Zechariah had posed: "How can I be sure of this? I am an old man and my wife is getting on in years." Zechariah was asking for proof that God could do what he promised; Mary was merely asking what God wanted her to do – she had promised her virginity to God, and she wanted to know if God was asking her something else. She didn't doubt God's wisdom or power; she just wanted more instructions. This is why the angel's response to her was generous, while his response to Zechariah was harsh. Zechariah answered God's call by saying, "Prove it to me"; Mary answered saying, "Show me the way to go."

We can learn no greater lesson than how to say yes to God. Mary's "yes" reversed Eve's "no," and paved the way for Christ's undoing of Adam's fall. Likewise, when God disrupts our lives – through the voice of conscience, the normal responsibilities and demands of our state in life, or the indications of Church teaching – our "yes" can echo Mary's and make more room for Christ in this fallen world. But our "no" – or even our "maybe" – can just as easily shut him out.

CHRIST THE FRIEND

Many friends exchange gifts, but only Christ has given us his own mother, to be our solace and our refuge as we strive to follow in his footsteps.

As he was dying on the cross, Jesus entrusted his mother to the care of his "beloved disciple," and he entrusted the disciple to her care: "When Jesus saw his mother and the disciple there whom he loved, he said to his mother, 'Woman, behold, your son.' Then he said to the disciple, 'Behold, your mother.' And from that hour the disciple took her into his home" (Jn 19:26-27).

From its earliest days, the Church has interpreted this passage in a deeply spiritual way: since Jesus has desired to have us as his brothers and sisters, he has also desired to share with us his mother, to give us a mother in the order of grace. Through the ages, Christians in all walks of life have been inspired by Mary's example, comforted by her spiritual solicitude, and aided by her heavenly intercession. Wherever one finds true devotion to Mary (which consists primarily in the imitation of her "yes" to God, not just in pious expressions and pretty pictures), one finds as well a passionate love for Jesus Christ, the Savior. She accompanied him on every step of his earthly sojourn, and she accompanies his little brothers and sisters (that's us) with equal love and concern.

CHRIST IN MY LIFE

Thank you for making me a Christian. You are the one Savior, the promised Messiah, and your Kingdom will have no end. You have called me into your Kingdom. What more could I ask for? You have given me your friendship. Lord, teach me to live closer to you, to have the same scale of values that you have, and to see all things with your eyes.

Mary, you were just a girl when God came and invited you to be the mother of the Savior. Even then you knew that God's will was the highest and wisest calling. You didn't fear missing out on all that the world had to offer, because you only wanted to stay close to the world's Creator. Teach me to trust and love Christ, and teach me to give him to others, as you gave him to us.

How strange, Lord, that you made the history of salvation depend not only on your own actions, but also on the free cooperation of your creatures! You waited for Mary to say yes before coming to be our Savior. You wait for each of us to say yes before coming to save us. I renew my "yes" right now. Teach me to help others say yes too; only what I do for your Kingdom will last forever.

Need we repeat what is the real
foundation of the dignity of
woman? It is precisely the same as
the foundation
of the dignity of man.
Both are children of God,
redeemed by Christ,
with the same
supernatural destiny.

POPE PIUS XII

The Uncongenial Family

The modern writers who have suggested, in a more or less open manner, that the family is a bad institution, have generally confined themselves to suggesting, with much sharpness, bitterness, or pathos, that perhaps the family not always very congenial. Of course the family is a good institution because it is uncongenial.

It is wholesome precisely because it contains so many divergencies and varieties. It is, as the sentimentalists say, like a little kingdom, and, like most other little kingdoms, is generally in a state of something resembling anarchy. It is exactly because our brother George is not interested in our religious difficulties, but is interested in the Trocadero restaurant, that the family has some of the bracing qualities of the commonwealth. It is precisely because our uncle Henry does not approve of the theatrical ambitions of our sister that that the family is like humanity.

The men and women who, for good reasons and bad, revolt against the family are, for good reasons and bad, simply revolting against mankind. Aunt Elizabeth is unreasonable, like mankind. Papa is excitable, like mankind. Our younger brother is mischievous, like mankind. Grandpapa is stupid, like the world; he is old, like the world.

G.K CHESTERTON, *HERETICS*

Motherhood always establishes a unique and unrepeatable relationship between two people: between mother and child and between child and mother. Even when the same woman is the mother of many children, her personal relationship with each one of them is the very essence of motherhood. For each child is generated in a unique and unrepeatable way. And this is true for both the mother and the child.

POPE JOHN PAUL II, *REDEMPTORIS MATER*

Glory Dawns

"By her maternal charity, Mary cares for the brethren of her Son who still wander through this world in the midst of dangers and difficulties until they are led to the happiness of their heavenly home."

SECOND VATICAN COUNCIL, LUMEN GENTIUM 61

JOHN 2:1-12

Three days later there was a wedding at Cana in Galilee. The mother of Jesus was there, and Jesus and his disciples had also been invited. When they ran out of wine, since the wine provided for the wedding was all finished, the mother of Jesus said to him, 'They have no wine.' Jesus said 'Woman, why turn to me? My hour has not come yet.' His mother said to the servants, 'Do whatever he tells you.' There were six stone water jars standing there, meant for the ablutions that are customary among the Jews: each could hold twenty or thirty gallons. Jesus said to the servants, 'Fill the jars with water,' and they filled them to the brim. 'Draw some out now' he told them 'and take it to the steward.' They did this; the steward tasted the water, and it had turned into wine. Having no idea where it came from – only the servants who had drawn the water knew – the steward called the bridegroom and said, 'People generally serve the best wine first, and keep the cheaper sort till the guests have had plenty to drink; but you have kept the best wine till now.' This was the first of the signs given by Jesus: it was given at Cana in Galilee. He let his glory be seen, and his disciples believed in him. After this he went down to Capernaum with his mother and the brothers, but they stayed there only a few days.

CHRIST THE LORD ❧

Mary knew how to treat the Lord: there was a crisis, and she went to him for a solution. The vast majority of Jews living in Palestine were poor. Wedding feasts and religious festivals were their sole respite from a life of hard labor and simple survival. In fact, wedding feasts often lasted for days at a time (they took the place of our honeymoons, which didn't exist in first-century Israel), and the entire town participated. To run out of wine in the middle of it would not only deflate the festive atmosphere, but it would also deeply shame the newlyweds and their families, turning what should be the most joyous days of their lives into an embarrassment. Attentive to the needs of those around her, Mary saw the crisis coming, and she knew just what to do. Even when the words of Jesus' answer seemed like a rebuff, she knew that he would come through. Jesus will never reject the humble appeal of faith – he is a Lord who "came not be served but to serve" (Mt 20:28), and he's hoping that we will have as much confidence in him as his mother did.

We shouldn't overlook the power Jesus shows in this miracle. It was the "first of his signs," and by it he "let his glory be seen," to the benefit of his disciples, whose faith it deepened. Picture what happened. Pretend you are one of the servants. You fill up six huge stone kegs with water (no easy task when you have to go back and forth to the well). Then this young rabbi from the neighboring town tells you to draw some out (some of the water, remember – you know it's water, because you put it in there yourself) and bring it to the steward in charge of testing the wine before serving it. Imagine how dumbfounded you would be by such an order. But you do it. And you're carrying the water over to the steward, glancing nervously back over your shoulder at Mary and Jesus, who motion for you to keep going. You hand the gourd to the boss, looking down, maybe even closing your eyes in anticipation of his wrathful rebuke. And then, all of a sudden, he smacks his lips and hums with pleasure.... Jesus turned a hundred gallons of water into excellent wine, effortlessly. This is our Lord.

CHRIST THE TEACHER

Jesus treated his mother with love and respect. He sees her not only as God's chosen instrument, but also as the woman who brought him into the world, took care of him when he was a helpless infant, and taught him to speak, to pray, to work, and to live. Both Jesus and Mary were free from sin, but that made them more human, not less. And so the natural, incomparable bond that forms between a mother and her son was deeper, purer, and more binding in their case than in any other case in human history. Since baptism has brought us into Christ's family, our love and respect for Mary should echo Christ's.

On the other hand, no one knows Jesus better than his mother. She bore him in her womb, nursed him at her breast, and raised him from childhood to manhood. Thirty of his thirty-three years on earth were spent in almost constant contact with her. When he begins his public ministry, she fades into the background but remains faithful: when he was in agony on the cross, she was there beside him. When she says something about him, therefore, we should take it to heart (just as he took to heart her hint that he should do something about the wine crisis), and in this passage she gives us an unambiguous lesson about how to relate to Jesus.

The Bible is inspired, so it is no coincidence that Mary's last biblical words say everything that needs to be said: "Do whatever he tells you." If we followed that one piece of advice, heeding Christ's every order and suggestion (those in the Scriptures, those of his Church, and those in our conscience), the water of our normal, everyday activities would quickly be turned into the wine of supernatural joy and fruitfulness. We would no longer be mere men and women; we would be saints.

CHRIST THE FRIEND

Jesus: I brought my disciples to a wedding feast. Think about that for a moment. Do you think it is something that happened by chance? Not at all. Too often people think of me as a stern taskmaster, distant and removed from the healthy joys and activities of the human experience. But I was the one who invented those joys and activities!

I came to earth not just to teach you theology and not to douse your zest for life, but to bring everything about life back to its fullness, back to its complete and rightly ordered fruition. I know much better than anyone else that it is part of human nature to celebrate, to enjoy the good things of creation, like marriage and wine. But only I can teach you how to do so in a balanced, healthy way, in a way that will deepen your joy and not cheapen it. Stay close to me, seek to know me better, and I will show you how to experience more fully the life I have given you.

CHRIST IN MY LIFE

Lord, I am so used to this miracle – too used to it. I have heard about it so many times. But when I stop to really reflect on what you did, I am amazed. Why do I live on the mundane surface of things so much? Why can't I keep in mind the wonders of your love, the gift of your presence, the assurance of your wisdom? You are all mine, Lord, and I am all yours. Keep me closer to your heart...

If I don't seek out and fulfill your will, whose will is left? Mine is ignorant and narrow-minded. No one else has your wisdom, love and fidelity. I want to know your will, your teaching, and your criteria. I want to learn to hear your voice. I want to live out all the normal responsibilities of my life as you would have me live them out, because I know that if I do, you will make my life bear abundant fruit...

I don't want to be one of those sad, cold, self-righteously pious, proper people. I want to be a saint, the saint you created me to be. The true saints, the ones your Church encourages me to look at, are so full of life that wherever they go they cause a revolution. Fill me with life, Lord, with your life, with true life. Make my words and my glance glow with the warmth of your love. Teach me to do your will...

Women are the only realists; their whole object in life is to pit their realism against the extravagant, excessive, and occasionally drunken idealism of men.

G. K. CHESTERTON

The Sun of the Family

The family has its own radiant sun, the wife. Hear how Scripture puts it:

> *The grace of a wife will charm her husband,*
> *Her accomplishments will make him the stronger.*
> *A silent wife is a gift from the Lord,*
> *No price can be put on a well-trained character.*
> *A modest wife is a boon twice over,*
> *A chaste character cannot be weighed on scales.*
> *Like the sun rising over the mountains of the Lord*
> *Is the beauty of a good wife in a well-kept house.*
>
> SIRACH 26:13-16

Yes; the wife and the mother is the radiant sun of the family. She is this sun by her generosity and gift of self, by her unfailing readiness, by her watchful and prudent delicacy in all matters which can add joy to the lives of her husband and her children. She spreads around her light and warmth. And if you can say that a marriage augurs well, when both partners seek the happiness of the other rather than their own, this noble feeling and intention is more especially the quality of the wife, although it concerns both husband and wife. It is born of the very pulse of her mother's heart and its wisdom; that wisdom which it if it receives bitterness, gives only joy; if it receives belittlement, returns only dignity and respect. It is like the sun which brightens the cloudy morning with its dawning ray and in its setting gilds the evening shower.

The wife is the radiant sun of the family with the brightness of her glance and the ardor of her word; a glance and a word which gently enter the soul, bending it and making it softer and lifting it out of the tumult of passion, and recalling her husband to joy in the good and in familiar conversation, after a long day of uninterrupted and often painful work, whether professional or agricultural, in commerce or in industry. The wife is the radiant sun of the family by her natural candor, by her simple dignity and by her Christian and decent behavior, as much by her collectedness of mind and uprightness of heart, as in the subtle harmony of her bearing and her dress, in her becomingness and in her behavior at once reserved and affectionate. Little signs of feeling, shades of facial expression, ingenuous silences and smiles, an approving movement of the head give to her the grace of some choice and yet simple flower which opens its petals to receive and reflect the colors of the sun.

If you could only know what deep feelings of affection and gratitude such an ideal wife and mother arouses and imprints in the hearts of her husbands and sons!

POPE PIUS XII, *ADDRESS TO NEWLY MARRIED COUPLES*, MARCH 11, 1942

Family Love

There's no vocabulary
For love within a family, love that's lived in
But not looked at, love within the light of which
All else is seen, the love within which
All other love finds speech.
This love is silent.

T.S. ELIOT

Reward

All day I did the little things,
The little things that do not show:
I brought the kindling for the fire
I set the candles in a row,
I filled a bowl with marigolds,
The shallow bowl you love the best –
And made the house a pleasant place
Where weariness might take its rest.

The hours sped on, my eager feet
Could not keep pace with my desire.
So much to do, so little time!
I could not let my body tire;
Yet, when the coming of the night
Blotted the garden from my sight,
And on the narrow, graveled walks
Between the guarding flower stalks
I heard your step: I was not through
With services I meant for you.

You came into the quiet room
That glowed enchanted with the bloom
Of yellow flame. I saw your face,
Illumined by the firelit space,
Slowly grow still and comforted –
"It's good to be at home," you said.

BLANCHE BANE KUDER

Quenching Christ's Thirst

> *"To show that he was not different from us, he*
> *undertake hard work, he went hungry and thirsty,*
> *he took rest and sleep, he did not shirk suffering, he*
> *revealed the Resurrection."*
>
> St Hippolytus

JOHN 4:1-30

When Jesus heard that the Pharisees had found out that he was making and baptising more disciples than John – though in fact it was his disciples who baptised, not Jesus himself – he left Judaea and went back to Galilee. This meant that he had to cross Samaria. On the way he came to the Samaritan town called Sychar, near the land that Jacob gave to his son Joseph. Jacob's well is there and Jesus, tired by the journey, sat straight down by the well. It was about the sixth hour. When a Samaritan woman came to draw water, Jesus said to her, 'Give me a drink.' His disciples had gone into the town to buy food. The Samaritan woman said to him, 'What? You are a Jew and you ask me, a Samaritan, for a drink?' – Jews, in fact, do not associate with Samaritans. Jesus replied: 'If you only knew what God is offering and who it is that is saying to you: Give me a drink, you would have been the one to ask, and he would have given you living water.'

'You have no bucket, sir,' she answered, 'and the well is deep: how could you get this living water? Are you a greater man than our father Jacob who gave us this well and drank from it himself with his sons and his cattle?' Jesus replied: 'Whoever drinks this water will get thirsty again; but anyone who drinks the water that I shall give will never be thirsty again: the water that I shall give will turn into a spring inside him, welling up to eternal life.' 'Sir,' said the woman 'give me some of that water, so that I may never get thirsty and never have to come here

*again to draw water.' 'Go and call your husband,' said Jesus
to her, 'and come back here.' The woman answered, 'I have
no husband.' He said to her, 'You are right to say, I have no
husband; for although you have had five, the one you have
now is not your husband. You spoke the truth there.' 'I see you
are a prophet, sir,' said the woman. 'Our fathers worshipped on
this mountain, while you say that Jerusalem is the place where
one ought to worship.'*

*Jesus said: 'Believe me, woman, the hour is coming when
you will worship the Father neither on this mountain nor in
Jerusalem. You worship what you do not know; we worship
what we do know: for salvation comes from the Jews. But
the hour will come – in fact it is here already – when true
worshippers will worship the Father in spirit and truth: that
is the kind of worshipper the Father wants. God is spirit, and
those who worship must worship in spirit and truth.' The
woman said to him, 'I know that Messiah – that is, Christ
– is coming; and when he comes he will tell us everything.' 'I
who am speaking to you,' said Jesus, 'I am he.' At this point his
disciples returned, and were surprised to find him speaking
to a woman, though none of them asked, 'What do you want
from her?' or, 'Why are you talking to her?' The woman put
down her water jar and hurried back to the town to tell the
people. 'Come and see a man who has told me everything I
ever did; I wonder if he is the Christ?' This brought people out
of the town and they started walking towards him.*

CHRIST THE LORD

Passing through Samaria was not the only route from
Judea to Galilee, but Jesus chose that route. He knew the
bigger picture. He is always attentive to our needs, just
as he was attentive to the needs of this woman and her

countrymen. He never uses his knowledge and power to oppress and abuse, but only to amplify his love.

Christ is the Savior of the World, the Messiah, the long-awaited King greater even than Jacob, inheritor of the Promise and father of the Twelve Tribes of Israel, so he tells this divorcee. He graces the Samaritan woman with one of the richest descriptions of himself and his work that appear in all the Scriptures. Why? Why tell so much to someone so insignificant? Because to him, she wasn't insignificant at all. He wanted to be known by her, to give her hope, to save her. Ours is a Lord who wishes to shower us with his love, to fill us with the "living waters" of "the Spirit and truth," and to "tell us everything." This is the God in whom we believe; this is the Lord we serve.

CHRIST THE TEACHER

Jesus was tired after his journey. He sat down by the well, thirsty, hungry, worn out. He was so thirsty that he skirted all social protocol and asked a Samaritan woman to give him a drink. But his tiredness doesn't hold back his love. He had come to rescue the lost sheep – this was his mission. The Samaritan woman came to the well at noon, the hottest hour of the day. The other women of the village would have come in the cooler hours of early morning and evening. This one was obviously avoiding contact with her peers. Jesus certainly notices this, seeing in her eyes the anxiety that comes from an unstable life, but he also sees a spark of sincerity – her rocky path through life had worn down any façade of self-righteousness or self-delusion. She was a woman in search of answers and direction, though she had perhaps given up on finding them. Jesus sees all this in her eyes, and he can't contain the love that overflows in his heart. He sees a soul in need, and he can't help reaching out. This is why he came.

Jesus became one of us on purpose with a mission in mind. Because of our sin, we could no longer raise ourselves up to friendship with God; so God comes down to meet us. In the Incarnation of Christ and the Church (which is the extension of that Incarnation throughout history) God continues to come down to meet us. He addresses us, he walks with us, he humbles himself so much that he even needs us to give him a drink: "Whatever you did for one of the least brothers of mine you did for me" (Mt 25:40). When the Samaritan woman encountered this God who was man, she was so transported with joy and so eager to spread the news that she forgot to bring back her water jar, the very reason she came to the well in the first place. Christ is the kind of friend who can make a real difference in our lives, one who can put things in perspective – if we let him.

CHRIST THE FRIEND ✒

The Samaritan woman: I knew something was different about that man as soon as I came up to the well. He looked at me in a way that men didn't usually look at me. I met his eyes for just a second, and then I looked away. But I wanted to look again. I had seen in his glance something that I had only dreamed about before: he knew me completely – he knew exactly what kind of person I was. Yet it didn't bother him; in fact, it was as if he was glad to see me – not because he wanted anything from me, but because he seemed to want something for me, as if he were pure kindness. So when I looked away, because that was the proper thing to do, I was just dying to look at him again, to see that kindness in his eyes, to drink it in.

But then I thought, no, it's only my imagination. And then he spoke to me. He asked me for a drink. And that was the beginning of a conversation that changed my life. I didn't understand everything he told me, but I understood that he knew me – he knew me through and through and he still cared about me, he was interested in me. For him, I

*was important, not just because I could give him something, but just...
well, just because. In his eyes, I mattered. Even then I knew that what
he said about being the Messiah was true. How else could I explain the
change that was already happening in my heart? It was as if a door had
opened in my life where before there had only been a thick, dark, high
wall protecting my broken heart. He freed me. I had to tell the others in
the town. I knew he was the Savior, and I just had to tell everyone. I
knew that as soon as they met him they too would realize it. And they
did! Before that day I was just surviving; after that encounter with his
words, his glance, his presence – from then on I began to live.*

CHRIST IN MY LIFE 🔊

Jesus, tell me everything. Tell me about myself and the
meaning of my life; tell me about your love and your wisdom and
your plan for my life. Lord, give me your living water – how thirsty
I am! I have tasted your gifts; I know at least a little bit about what
you are offering. I want to know more. I want to live closer to you.
I want to lead others to your heart, just as you led me...

I believe in you, Lord, and in your eagerness to save souls
who are stuck in sin and darkness. And I believe that you can
save them, just as you turned this woman's life around – just
as you have turned my life around. Thank you for guiding
me. Thank you for not giving up on me. Thank you for giving
me a mission in life...

What does it mean, Lord, to worship in "Spirit and truth"?
You want it; you came to make it possible. To worship is to
acknowledge your greatness, majesty, and goodness. You want
me to do so not only in external ceremonies but in my heart,
in my attitudes, in my choices. You want me to live as you
would have me live, Lord, trusting in you, seeking your will
always. Teach me to do so, because this is what you desire...

An email from Uncle Eddy about St Gianna Beretta Molla
(Feast Day, April 28, entered heaven on that day in 1962)

Dear Joan,

I think you're creating unnecessary dilemmas. You're about to enter into the professional world. You have a good education behind you, plenty of opportunity, a strong faith, and a healthy social life. I don't see why you think that professional success can only be had if you decide not to get married. It's not an "either or" situation, necessarily. As long as you keep Christ first and decide to follow his will no matter what, you can't go wrong. Take today's saint, for example.

Gianna was from Milan, Italy. She is famous as the "pro-life" saint, because when serious complications in her fifth pregnancy arose, she insisted to her husband and her doctor that everything should be done to save her child, regardless of what happened to her. Friends tried to dissuade her, pointing out that she had other children to take care of, but she said, "I must fulfill my duty as a mother..." meaning, of course, that she must give life to her child. Even Church moralists agreed that she would be acting morally if she allowed the doctors to try and remove her ovarian cyst, although the operation would put the child at a risk. But she insisted that everything be done in favor of her daughter, who was born, healthy, at midnight on Holy Saturday, 1962. For the following week Gianna suffered unspeakable pain as internal bleeding and other complications poisoned her system until she died, only forty years old.

That much most people know, and that's enough to demonstrate the heroic virtue that saints must show. But few know about the rest of her life. She was, in so many ways, a normal, modern woman. She excelled in her studies and became a medical doctor. Her husband was a successful businessman who traveled extensively, and yet together they formed a healthy, happy home life with their four children. She loved to ski, to go to the theatre. She followed the latest fashions and traveled with her husband as frequently as possible. She was fun-loving, outgoing, good-looking... She was a lot like you. And her holiness, which didn't spontaneously appear all of a sudden in the midst of her crisis, but was cultivated throughout her life, only added joy and energy to this holy woman of the world.

And that's my point. What the world and the Church need today more than ever are integral Christians, Christians who live in the world with joy and simplicity and normality, and yet whose love for Christ informs everything they do. This is essential to bringing Christ and his grace to the spiritually starving world. Don't you think that Christ is calling more young women to follow in St Gianna's footsteps? Do you think maybe he's calling you there? Listen closely, and go wherever he tells you.

Your loving uncle,

Eddy

P.S. You may want to memorize St Gianna's favorite prayer:

*Jesus, I promise You to submit myself to all that You permit
to befall me; make me only know Your will. My most sweet Jesus,
infinitely merciful God, most tender Father of souls, and in a
particular way of the most weak, most miserable, most infirm
which You carry with special tenderness between Your divine
arms, I come to You to ask You, through the love and merits of Your
Sacred Heart, the grace to comprehend and to do always Your holy
will, the grace to confide in You, the grace to rest securely
through time and eternity in Your loving divine arms.*

The Snowstorm

The cold wind swept the mountain's height,
And pathless was the dreary wild,
And mid the cheerless hours of night
A mother wandered with her child.

As through the drifted snows she pressed,
The babe was sleeping on her breast,
The babe was sleeping on her breast.

And colder still the winds did blow,
And darker hours of night came on,
And deeper grew the drifts of snow--
Her limbs were chilled, her strength was gone.

"O God!" she cried, in accents wild,
"If I must perish, save my child,
"If I must perish save my child."

She stript her mantle from her breast,
And bared her bosom to the storm;
As round the child she wrapped the vest,
She smiled to think that it was warm.

With one cold kiss, one tear she shed,
And sunk upon a snowy bed,
And sunk upon a snowy bed.

At dawn, a traveller passed by,
And saw her 'neath a snowy veil--
The frost of death was in her eye,
Her cheek was cold, and hard and pale--

He moved the robe from off the child;
The babe looked up, and sweetly smiled,
The babe looked up, and sweetly smiled.

SEBA SMITH

Mary's Song

"The Holy Spirit heated, inflamed and melted
Mary with love, as fire does iron, so that the
flame of the Spirit was seen and nothing was
felt but the fire of the love of God."

St Ildefonsus of Toledo

LUKE 1:39-56

*Mary set out at that time and went as quickly as she could
to a town in the hill country of Judah. She went into Zechariah's
house and greeted Elizabeth. Now as soon as Elizabeth heard
Mary's greeting, the child leapt in her womb and Elizabeth was
filled with the Holy Spirit. She gave a loud cry and said, 'Of all
women you are the most blessed, and blessed is the fruit of your
womb. Why should I be honoured with a visit from the mother
of my Lord? For the moment your greeting reached my ears, the
child in my womb leapt for joy. Yes, blessed is she who believed
that the promise made her by the Lord would be fulfilled.' And
Mary said: 'My soul proclaims the greatness of the Lord, and
my spirit exults in God my saviour; because he has looked upon
his lowly handmaid. Yes, from this day forward all generations
will call me blessed, for the Almighty has done great things for
me. Holy is his name, and his mercy reaches from age to age for
those who fear him. He has shown the power of his arm, he has
routed the proud of heart. He has pulled down princes from their
thrones and exalted the lowly. The hungry he has filled with good
things, the rich sent empty away. He has come to the help of Israel
his servant, mindful of his mercy – according to the promise he
made to our ancestors – of his mercy to Abraham and to his
descendants for ever.' Mary stayed with Elizabeth about three
months and then went back home.*

CHRIST THE LORD

Elizabeth knows what's going on. After years of infertility, God has seen fit to make her the mother of John the Baptist, the Messiah's herald, whom she is still carrying in her womb. In response to such a privilege she has drawn closer to God, filled as she is with humble gratitude and a new appreciation of his mercy and generosity. Therefore, God begins to fill her with the Holy Spirit, who in turn keeps drawing her deeper into the mysterious and wonderful events taking place through and around her. This intimate union with God enables her to perceive God's presence in Christ, even though he is only an embryo in Mary's womb. And she calls him "my Lord."

Before he ever worked any wonders, before he mesmerized the crowds with his preaching, before he rose from the dead, indeed, from all eternity, Jesus is "the Lord."

CHRIST THE TEACHER

It's impossible to tell the story of Christmas without including Mary. As Christ's first and most faithful disciple, the first one to welcome him into the world, she shows all of us how to live every Advent and Christmas season – indeed, every season of our Christian life – with faith. Through her example, Christ teaches us how to respond to God's action in and around us: by believing in him and by trusting that whatever he may be asking of us is the best available option.

Who are we to argue with God, to disobey him? Will he deceive us? Will he lead us astray? Mary, partially enlightened by her heartfelt knowledge of God's plan as revealed in the Old Testament scriptures, could not see clearly how God's plans would work themselves out in the end. Even so, humbly and trustingly she put her faith in them, and for that wise faith she was "blessed among women," as Elizabeth exclaimed. The Lord is constantly hoping that we will put our trust in him in the same way, so that he can shower his blessings upon us as well.

What was Mary's secret? Why was she able to believe so firmly and to fulfill her vocation so magnificently? Why did she succeed where Eve had failed? She reveals her secret in this hymn of praise that bursts from her heart as soon as she greets Elizabeth.

During the whole journey from Nazareth to the hill country outside Jerusalem where Elizabeth and Zechariah lived, she had been joyfully contemplating all that God had done in her life and in the whole history of salvation. When she meets Elizabeth and realizes that God has revealed his plans to her as well, she feels free to give full expression to her thoughts and sentiments.

She sings the *Magnificat*, a prayer that still echoes throughout the world every day through the liturgy of the Church. In its simple words, imbued with the prayers of the Old Testament, we glimpse Mary's vision of reality, in which God rules all things with perfect power and with a wisdom that confounds the vain ambition of men. Humility, a serene recognition of our utter dependence on God, unleashes the power of divine grace in the world. Those who depend on themselves – the rich, the self-satisfied, the proud, the powerful – thwart God's action in and through them. This is Mary's secret – and it is a secret no longer. She teaches it to all who are willing to learn.

CHRIST THE FRIEND

God is already caring for us long before we realize it. He has had a plan in mind for us, a particular vocation, a unique role in his Kingdom, from before we were born, before we were ever conceived. In discovering and living out that plan we find our true and lasting joy. Why else is John the Baptist able to "leap for joy" while he is still in his mother's womb? Only because God had made him the herald, the precursor, the one who would announce the imminent manifestation of the Messiah – this was his God-given mission in life, his vocation. Before he is aware of it, he is already fulfilling it.

Likewise, before we hear God's call in our life, he is already preparing us to follow it – and hoping that when the call comes we will respond generously, so that he can make our hearts leap continually with joy until he welcomes us into his heavenly Kingdom.

CHRIST IN MY LIFE

Lord, are you still at work in the world the way you were back when these wonderful happenings were unfolding? I know you are. I know that every time Mass is celebrated, it's a new Annunciation, a new Bethlehem, a new Calvary. I know that you never cease drawing us to yourself. Open my eyes, increase my faith! I want to see you at work in all things...

Humility is a mystery to me, Lord. How humble Mary must have been! Unspoiled, uncontaminated by original sin and the slew of selfish tendencies it sets loose in our souls! Mary, my Mother, teach me your secret. Teach me to be truly humble, truly great in God's eyes, so that my life will bear fruit for Christ's Kingdom...

Lord, I know that you really do have something in mind for me. You created me to know you and love you as only I can. My concept of my vocation may not be in perfect sync with yours. But even so, I want to follow you. I want to discover and fulfill your will for me. I want to perceive it and understand it more deeply every day, so that I can embrace it more fully each moment...

Woman: God's Best Gift to Man

"A great gift I could not give man.

And when I sent my Son on earth, he was not hard to please.

No, he was not hard to please – either about food, or lodging, or state in life, or about anything, except his Mother. But about her he was exacting.

He wanted his mother to be a masterpiece, surpassing even my angels, who are already very great masterpieces.

Yes, for her he was exacting – for the woman who was to bring him into the world and awaken his soul and form his heart.

And men are like him. Choosing a woman is always the great affair of their life.

Which doesn't surprise me,"

Says God.

HENRI GODIN

The Wisdom of Mothers

This *mutual gift of the person in marriage* opens to the gift of a new life, *a new human being,* who is also a person in the likeness of his parents. Motherhood implies from the beginning a special openness to the new person: and this is precisely the woman's "part." In this openness, in conceiving and giving birth to a child, the woman "discovers herself through a sincere gift of self." The gift of interior readiness to accept the child and bring it into the world is linked to the marriage union, which – as mentioned earlier – should constitute a special moment in the mutual self-giving both by the woman and the man.

According to the Bible, the conception and birth of a new human being are accompanied by the following words of the woman: "I have brought a man into being with the help of the Lord" (Gn 4:1). This exclamation of Eve, the "mother of all the living" is repeated every time a new human being comes into the world. It expresses the woman's joy and awareness that she is sharing in the great mystery of eternal generation. The spouses share in the creative power of God!

Motherhood involves a special communion with the mystery of life, as it develops in the woman's womb. The mother is filled with wonder at this mystery of life, and "understands" with unique intuition what is happening inside her. In the light of the "beginning," the mother accepts and loves as a person the child she is carrying in her womb. This unique contact with the new human being developing within her gives rise to an attitude towards human beings – not only towards her own child, but every human being – which profoundly marks the woman's personality. It is commonly thought that *women* are more capable than men of paying attention *to another person,* and that motherhood develops this predisposition even more.

The man – even with all his sharing in parenthood – always remains "outside" the process of pregnancy and the baby's birth; in many ways he has to *learn* his own *"fatherhood" from the mother.* One can say that this is part of the normal human dimension of parenthood, including the stages that follow the birth of the baby, especially the initial period. The child's upbringing, taken as a whole, should include the contribution of both parents: the maternal and paternal contribution. In any event, the mother's contribution is decisive in laying the foundation for a new human personality.

POPE JOHN PAUL II, *MULIERIS DIGNITATEM,* 18

Women have a thirst for order and beauty as for something physical; there is a strange female power of hating ugliness and waste as good men can only hate sin and bad men virtue.

G.K. CHESTERTON

Love Conquers Death

"He was indeed the true God and hence brought it about that the blind saw, the lame walked, the deaf heard, he cleansed those afflicted with leprosy, and by a simple command called the dead back to life."

ST GREGORY AGRIGENTINUS

LUKE 7:11-17

Now soon afterwards he went to a town called Nain, accompanied by his disciples and a great number of people. When he was near the gate of the town it happened that a dead man was being carried out for burial, the only son of his mother, and she was a widow. And a considerable number of the townspeople were with her. When the Lord saw her he felt sorry for her. 'Do not cry,' he said. Then he went up and put his hand on the bier and the bearers stood still, and he said, 'Young man, I tell you to get up.' And the dead man sat up and began to talk, and Jesus gave him to his mother. Everyone was filled with awe and praised God saying, 'A great prophet has appeared among us; God has visited his people.' And this opinion of him spread throughout Judaea and all over the countryside.

CHRIST THE LORD

Jesus commands a dead man to rise, and he is obeyed. He shows that he is the Lord of life. And yet, when he commands us, "Do unto others as you would have them do unto you," or "Do not worry about tomorrow," or "Follow me," we resist. Does his Lordship work only on the dead?

Hardly. Rather, he refuses to force his way into our hearts; he is Lord, but he is also Love. He makes his Lordship known, and then he invites us to fight under his banner – but there are no mercenaries in his army, only friends who serve the Lord of Love out of love for the Lord.

When he asks us something difficult, we should remember this passage. The same power which raised this dead man to life is at work in his commands to us. In baptism, this power floods our soul with grace through the words of the priest and the sign of water. In confession, this same power cleanses and renews our souls. Every word that Jesus speaks to us has the power to raise us up, to lift us into the kind of life we long to live.

CHRIST THE TEACHER

The lesson is so simple that we may miss it: God cares. "Do not cry," he tells the woman, as if to say, "I can't bear to see you suffer. Let me help." No one asked him to perform this miracle – not even his disciples, who should have. The same motive behind his journey from heaven to earth through the Incarnation moves him to comfort this lonely widow. And the same motive is behind everything else he did before that moment and everything he accomplished since then: he cares. Such a simple lesson – but one that's so easy to forget!

Another more subtle lesson is hidden in this passage as well. The woman was a widow, like Jesus' own mother, Mary. (Joseph had died, tradition tells us, before Jesus set out on his public ministry.) The woman had only one son, again like Mary. Mary too will watch her only son die and be buried. Jesus' reaching out to this suffering woman reveals one of the most attractive characteristics of his Sacred Heart: his truly filial love for his Mother. How could Mary not have an entirely unique place in the perfect heart of the Redeemer? The Church's ancient practice of invoking Mary's intercession is, in this sense, an act of reverence made to Christ's Incarnation: only because he shares completely our humanity does he have a mother in the first place, and because faithful sons honor and respect their mothers – all the more so when the son is a perfect King and the mother a wise and selfless Queen – Jesus gives Mary a throne at his side. And just as he couldn't resist the heart's desire of this weeping widow of Nain, how can he resist Mary's heartfelt intercession on our behalf?

CHRIST THE FRIEND

We never have to suffer alone. Some time before, the widow had lost her husband, and now she loses her only son; she certainly must have felt as alone as a person can feel, inconsolable in her grief even while surrounded by the crowd. Who can fathom the depths of a mother's love? And yet, she found someone who shared her pain – Jesus. Not only did he perceive her moral agony, her utter loneliness, but he had compassion on her; he suffered *with* her (which is what the word compassion means). Because of this, he knew how to relieve her suffering; when he came over to her and placed her resurrected son's hand in hers, she was no longer alone.

Sometimes we do feel like we are suffering alone – Christ seems far away; at least he doesn't intervene so dramatically as he did in Nain. But indulging such feelings shows a lack of faith. This poor widow did not know about Calvary; she had never seen a crucifix. The only way Christ had to show her his compassion was to restore her son to life. But we have seen Calvary. We know to what depths God's compassion has gone. And we can always go to the Tabernacle, where we find the Eucharist, the living memorial of Calvary – the revelation of God's unfathomable compassion, his "suffering with" each and every one of us. Truly, we never have to suffer alone. And so, when we choose to do so anyway, we not only increase our own pain, but we double Christ's as well, by turning a blind eye to his cross.

CHRIST IN MY LIFE

Lord, I know I have to obey someone in life: either myself, with all my ignorance and limitations, or some other teacher or guru, or the shallow advice of popular culture (which only cares about turning me into a good consumer) – or you. I want to obey you. I choose once again to follow you. Lord Jesus, I believe that you are the way, the truth, and the life...

I know that you are with me in every moment of my life, the good moments and the bad ones. You suffer with me, because you know that having to suffer alone would double my pain. Why do I insist on walking alone? Why do I insist on resisting your compassion and comfort and the soothing balm of your Church's doctrine? Jesus, teach me to bear my cross with you...

Mary, you are my mother as well as Christ's, because my baptism made me a child of God. Teach me to be like Jesus. Teach me to trust in him, to know his goodness and his power so deeply that I never doubt him – so that I never fall back into self-absorption and angry frustration. Teach me to be bold and faithful ambassador of his Kingdom. Queen of peace, pray for me...

Home Sweet Home

Mid pleasures and palaces though we may roam,
Be it ever so humble, there's no place like home;
A charm from the sky seems to hallow us there,
Which, seek through the world, is ne'er met with elsewhere.
Home, Home, sweet, sweet Home!
There's no place like Home! there's no place like Home!

An exile from home, splendor dazzles in vain;
O, give me my lowly thatched cottage again!
The birds singing gayly, that came at my call,--
Give me them,--and the peace of mind, dearer than all!
Home, Home, sweet, sweet Home!
There's no place like Home! there's no place like Home!

How sweet 'tis to sit 'neath a fond father's smile,
And the cares of a mother to soothe and beguile!
Let others delight mid new pleasures to roam,
But give me, oh, give me, the pleasures of home!
Home, Home, sweet, sweet Home!
There's no place like Home! there's no place like Home!

To thee I'll return, overburdened with care;
The heart's dearest solace will smile on me there;
No more from that, cottage again will I roam;
Be it ever so humble, there's no place like home.
Home, Home, sweet, sweet Home!
There's no place like Home! there's no place like Home!

JOHN HOWARD PAYNE

A Mother's Contagious Courage

But the mother was especially admirable and worthy of honourable remembrance, for she watched the death of seven sons in the course of a single day, and bravely endured it because of her hopes in the Lord. Indeed she encouraged each of them in their ancestral tongue; filled with noble conviction, she reinforced her womanly argument with manly courage, saying to them, "I do not know how you appeared in my womb; it was not I who endowed you with breath and life, I had not the shaping of your every part. And hence, the Creator of the world, who made everyone and ordained the origin of all things, will in his mercy give you back breath and life, since for the sake of his laws you have no concern for yourselves."

Antiochus thought he was being ridiculed, suspecting insult in the tone of her voice; and as the youngest was still alive he appealed to him not with mere words but with promises on oath to make him both rich and happy if he would abandon the traditions of his ancestors; he would make him his friend and entrust him with public office. The young man took no notice at all, and so the king then appealed to the mother, urging her to advise the youth to save his life. After a great deal of urging on his part she agreed to try persuasion on her son.

Bending over him, she fooled the cruel tyrant with these words, uttered in their ancestral tongue, "My son, have pity on me; I carried you nine months in my womb and suckled you three years, fed you and reared you to the age you are now, and provided for you. I implore you, my child, look at the earth and sky and everything in them, and consider how God made them out of what did not exist, and that human beings come into being in the same way. Do not fear this executioner, but prove yourself worthy of your brothers and accept death, so that I may receive you back with them in the day of mercy."

She had hardly finished, when the young man said, "What are you all waiting for? I will not comply with the king's ordinance; I obey the ordinance of the Law given to our ancestors through Moses… I too, like my brothers, surrender my body and life for the laws of my ancestors, begging God quickly to take pity on our nation, and by trials and afflictions to bring you to confess that he alone is God…"

The king fell into a rage and treated this one more cruelly than the others, for he was himself smarting from the young man's scorn. And so the last brother met his end undefiled and with perfect trust in the Lord. The mother was the last to die, after her sons.

2 MACCABEES 7:20-41

You cannot teach what you do not know
yourselves. Teach them to love God,
to love Christ, to love our Mother
the Church and the pastors
of the Church who are
your guides.
Love the catechism
and teach your children
to love it; it is the great
handbook of the love
and fear of God, of Christian
wisdom and of eternal life.

POPE PIUS XII

In Partnership with Grace

"Obedience is the backbone of faith."

ST FRANCIS OF PAOLA

LUKE 8:1-15

Now after this he made his way through towns and villages preaching, and proclaiming the Good News of the kingdom of God. With him went the Twelve, as well as certain women who had been cured of evil spirits and ailments: Mary surnamed the Magdalene, from whom seven demons had gone out, Joanna the wife of Herod's steward Chuza, Susanna, and several others who provided for them out of their own resources. With a large crowd gathering and people from every town finding their way to him, he used this parable: 'A sower went out to sow his seed. As he sowed, some fell on the edge of the path and was trampled on; and the birds of the air ate it up. Some seed fell on rock, and when it came up it withered away, having no moisture. Some seed fell amongst thorns and the thorns grew with it and choked it. And some seed fell into rich soil and grew and produced its crop a hundredfold.' Saying this he cried, 'Listen, anyone who has ears to hear!' His disciples asked him what this parable might mean, and he said, The mysteries of the kingdom of God are revealed to you; for the rest there are only parables, so that they may see but not perceive, listen but not understand 'This, then, is what the parable means: the seed is the word of God. Those on the edge of the path are people who have heard it, and then the devil comes and carries away the word from their hearts in case they should believe and be saved. Those on the rock are people who, when they first hear it, welcome the word with joy. But these have no root; they believe for a while, and in time of trial they give up. As for the part that fell into thorns, this is people who have heard, but as they go on their way they are choked by the worries and riches and pleasures of life and do not reach maturity. As for the part in the rich soil, this is people with a noble and generous heart who have heard the word and take it to themselves and yield a harvest through their perseverance.

CHRIST THE LORD

Jesus is humble. He has all knowledge and all power, and he wants to give us a share for our happiness and salvation, but he constantly shows an attentive respect for our freedom. The passage illustrates this characteristic respect in two ways.

First, St Luke has Jesus start using parables. A parable presents a truth in brilliant clarity, but leaves it up to the listener to apply that truth to his own life. Jesus wants us to do this, saying, "Listen, anyone who has ears to hear!" At the same time, he knows that many who hear him are so attached to their own ideas and way of living that they are not really looking for wisdom, and so they will not search the parable for how it applies to their lives – "They may see but not perceive, listen but not understand..." If Jesus had taught more directly, those who were eager to learn would have assimilated it less completely – because when we have to make an effort to understand, we learn more deeply – and those who were just hanging around to see the show would have been immediately turned off, losing even the small chance they had of getting hit by a stray spark of grace.

Second, the parable itself reveals God's astonishing methodology of salvation. His grace is the seed, and our souls are the soil. Without the soil, the seed is completely useless. But without the seed, the soil is utterly barren. Each is made for each other. God's grace cannot work in our lives unless we receive it with a "noble and generous heart," unless we recognize our need for God, even if only in a vague and partial way, and seek his guidance. But no matter how intensely we may be seeking answers and wisdom and meaning, unless God intervenes with his grace, we will remain completely in the dark, like the barren blackness of a lifeless field.

How humble the Lord is to enter into an equal partnership with the very sinners who banished his grace from their souls!

CHRIST THE TEACHER

God always supplies his grace. He always does his part in our spiritual lives. We can count on it. But we don't always do our part. Our attitude towards God's will determines the fate of his grace. If we are "noble and generous," his grace will have plenty of room to fill our lives with the fruits of holiness and happiness. If we give up when God's will requires us to persevere through tough times, his grace will wither. If we try to two-time God and the world, as if the cares and pleasures of life on earth were on an equal footing with our friendship with Christ, his grace will be sterile. Unless we make God's will – especially as discerned in our conscience and through Church teaching – our highest priority, we aren't really letting God be God, and so he can't make our life what he created it to be.

But the parable has yet another lesson. The first obstacle to God's grace appears to be the devil – represented by the birds that pick the seed up off the path. Actually, however, the occasion that gives the devil a chance to get in there is, once again, due to the quality of the soil, the attitudes of our soul. The soil on the path is hardened. The seed can't sink in. This is the superficial soul, the person who never takes time to reflect, to pray, to think deeply, the person who lets himself be "distracted from distractions by distractions," as T. S. Eliot put it. In a culture more and more dominated by information and mass media, this is perhaps the greatest danger of all. The constant flow of images, ideas, opinions, advertisements, chats, noise, music, entertainment, news, and everything else can, if we let it, create such a quantity of traffic in our minds that we become unable to savor truth, even on the off chance that we recognize it amidst the din. The same mind we use all day long, the one we fill with idle chatter and sensationalized news and everything else – that's the same mind we bring to prayer. Unless we put a fence around what we attend to in our minds, unless we practice self-mastery and discipline in our thoughts, the graces God constantly sends us will bounce onto the top of the beaten track and sit there, easy pickings for the devil.

CHRIST THE FRIEND 🔖

Susanna: Many things were different about Jesus. His words, his miracles, his presence.... But from the very first time I met him, what struck me most was how he treated women. He had no fear of us, and he put on no airs of superiority or false dignity. He treated us as equals. He knew us. He respected us. He let us help him and take care of him. With Jesus we were colleagues; we shared in his projects, in his work. And we were also friends, because we shared his needs. He depended on us. He chose to need us. In him, I learned that real friendship with God is possible. All distances collapsed. Much later, after he had risen from the dead and gone back to his Father, some of the disciples were frightened and, well, confused and hesitant. Mary told us then that we should be afraid of nothing; he left us with a mission, because he wanted to continue in our friendship. He left his Kingdom in our hands because he wanted to continue needing us. He gave us the most precious gift he could think of: he entrusted to us the task of leading others into eternal life. For Jesus, everyone mattered; everyone was worthy.

CHRIST IN MY LIFE

I want to kneel down and thank you for being so patient with me. You want to save me, but not at the cost of obliterating my humanity. How wise you are, Lord! But how slow and distracted I am in response to your wisdom! Teach me, Jesus; I want to learn the secrets of your Kingdom. I have ears, and I want to hear you, but I need you to take me by the hand, every day...

Once and for all, Lord, I want to take control of how I use the mass media. My spiritual progress depends on it. Help me, guide me, teach me, somehow show me the way to make good use of these wonderful inventions, which you surely want to be put at the service of our good, but which are so easy to abuse. Give me the strength of will and mind to guard the soil of my heart...

Thank you for coming into my life. Lord, I think of the thousands, maybe millions, of people who don't know you, who don't know that they can be friends with God and sharers in your incomparable mission. Send messengers to bring them your truth and grace! Send me! I want to want what you want, to do what you want, to want what you do...

The Reading Mother

I had a mother who read to me
Sagas of pirates who scoured the sea,
Cutlasses clenched in their yellow teeth,
"Blackbirds" stowed in the hold beneath.

I had a Mother who read me lays
Of ancient and gallant and golden days;
Stories of Marmion and Ivanhoe,
Which every boy has a right to know.

I had a Mother who read me tales
Of Gelert the hound of the hills of Wales,
True to his trust till his tragic death,
Faithfulness blent with his final breath.

I had a Mother who read me the things
That wholesome life to the boy heart brings
Stories that stir with an upward touch,
Oh, that each mother of boys were such!

You may have tangible wealth untold
Caskets of jewels and coffers of gold.
Richer than I you can never be –
I had a Mother who read to me.

STRICKLAND GILLIAN

*Judicious mothers will always keep in mind, that they are the
first book read, and the last put aside, in every child's library.*

C. LENOX REDMOND

Mother: A Personal Trainer for the Soul

Train the mind of your children. Do not give them wrong ideas or wrong reasons for things. Whatever their questions may be, do not answer them with evasions or untrue statements, which their minds rarely accept, but take occasion from them lovingly and patiently to train their minds, which want only to open to the truth and to grasp it with the first ingenuous gropings of their reasoning and reflective powers. Who can say what many a genius may not owe to the prolonged and trustful questionings of a childhood at the home fireside!

Train the character of your children. Correct their faults, encourage and cultivate their good qualities and coordinate them with that stability which will make for resolution in after life. Your children, conscious as they grow up and as they begin to think and will, that they are guided by a good parental will, constant and strong, free from violence and anger, not subject to weakness or inconsistency, will learn in time to see therein the interpreter of another and higher will, the will of God, and so they will plant in their souls the seeds of those early moral habits which fashion and sustain character, train it to self-control in moments of crisis and to courage in the face of conflict or sacrifice, and imbue it with a deep sense of Christian duty.

Train their hearts. Frequently the decision of a man's destiny, the ruin of his character or a grave danger threatening him may be traced to his childish years when his heart was spoiled by the fond flattery, silly fussing, and foolish indulgence of misguided parents. The impressionable little heart became accustomed to see all things revolve and gravitate around it, to find all things yielding to its will and caprice, and so there took root in it that boundless egoism of which the parents themselves were later to become the first victims.

POPE PIUS XII, *ADDRESS TO WOMEN OF CATHOLIC ACTION*, OCTOBER 26, 1941

Woman, the crown of creation , and in a certain sense its masterpiece; woman, that gentle creature to whose delicate hands God seems to have entrusted the future of the world to such an extent, in so far as she is man's help; woman, the expression of all that is best, kindest, most lovable here below...

POPE PIUS XII

Fearless Faith

"Christ has dominion over all creatures, a dominion not seized by violence nor usurped, but his by essence and by nature."

ST CYRIL OF ALEXANDRIA

LUKE 8:16-25

'No one lights a lamp to cover it with a bowl or to put it under a bed. No, he puts it on a lamp-stand so that people may see the light when they come in. For nothing is hidden but it will be made clear, nothing secret but it will be known and brought to light. So take care how you hear; for anyone who has will be given more; from anyone who has not, even what he thinks he has will be taken away.' His mother and his brothers came looking for him, but they could not get to him because of the crowd. He was told, 'Your mother and brothers are standing outside and want to see you.' But he said in answer, 'My mother and my brothers are those who hear the word of God and put it into practice'. One day, he got into a boat with his disciples and said to them, 'Let us cross over to the other side of the lake.' So they put to sea, and as they sailed he fell asleep. When a squall came down on the lake the boat started taking in water and they found themselves in danger. So they went to rouse him saying, 'Master! Master! We are going down!' Then he woke up and rebuked the wind and the rough water; and they subsided and it was calm again. He said to them, 'Where is your faith?' They were awestruck and astonished and said to one another, 'Who can this be, that gives orders even to winds and waves and they obey him?'

CHRIST THE LORD ☙

Imagine how the disciples would have remembered this event. It must have left a particularly deep impression on them. So many of them were fishermen, experts in working a boat and navigating rough waters. And yet in the face of this squall, they panic. It must have been a terrible storm. It must have been humbling for them to admit that their experience and skill failed them, but fail they did.

We are all fragile and small, no matter how much success we may have experienced in life. Sooner or later we have to face this truth, and when we do, we should follow the example of the apostles. They did the right thing when their resources ran out – they went to the Master. He is always near, even if he seems asleep. And no storm is too great for his calming touch. In fact, the most elemental and uncontrollable powers of nature, in the face of which even modern technology has to bow its proud head, meekly obey the word of the Lord.

Some spiritual writers see in this passage a prequel to the Resurrection. Jesus asleep in the boat anticipates his sleep of death in the tomb. The storm corresponds to the fears and doubts that beset the scattered disciples after the tragedy of the cross. Jesus waking up and calming the wind and water is his resurrection on the third day, which renews the apostles' confidence. In the face of our own storms, we should make a point of keeping the Lord's resurrection in mind – it's our lifetime warranty and everlasting guarantee.

CHRIST THE TEACHER ☙

The light of Christ's doctrine, which is only penetrating the apostles' hearts bit by bit as they have a chance to question him in private about his parables and teachings, will one day shine out for the whole world to see, through the work of the Church. And throughout the epoch of the Church, Christ's disciples are called to boldly spread that light. He has given it to us for our own good, but also so that we in turn will light up the whole household of mankind.

Jesus related this parable of the lamp because he knew we would be tempted to keep what we have received to ourselves. We hide things under bowls and under beds when we are afraid that other people will see them. When it comes to our Christian beliefs, fear of mockery, disdain, and rejection often make us hesitate when we should speak forth. The possibility of persecution throws us into a panic, just as the storm on the lake threw the apostles into a panic. The solution for our cowardice is the same as the solution Christ gave the apostles – faith: "Where is your faith?" God has given us more than enough reasons to believe in him and trust in him – now we just have to exercise the little faith we already have, and it will soon grow into a robust, joyful, and fruitful virtue: "Anyone who has will be given more." Otherwise, hiding the lamp under a bowl may protect the lamp, but it will snuff out the flame; our timorous efforts to avoid ridicule and persecution will have deprived even our own lives of Christ's saving light: "From anyone who has not, even what he thinks he has will be taken away."

CHRIST THE FRIEND

In this passage, Jesus reiterates his Kingdom's fundamental law of generosity, the only law that makes sense in a Kingdom where all the King's subjects are also his friends, brothers, and sisters. He states this law in a slightly different way than he has before by saying, "Anyone who has will be given more" – a little trust and obedience can quickly grow into an abundant harvest of all the virtues. Then he points to a living illustration: Mary, his mother. She and some of his relatives have come looking for him, and Jesus makes the most of the opportunity to remind his listeners of what he really wants for them. He came to earth to atone for our sins and win us a place inside God's family. If only we trust him enough to fulfil God's will, to live as Jesus teaches we should live, "hearing the word of God and putting it into practice," then we will become his very brothers and sisters and mothers.

This is exactly what had happened with Mary. She trusted in God; she lived with the consciousness of being "the handmaid of the Lord" (Lk 1:38). And because of her faith, God was able to give her much more; he made her into the mother of the Lord. From handmaid to mother, from village girl to Queen of the Universe – this is the "anyone who has will be given more" rule at its best, and Jesus wants us to give him a chance to apply it in our lives as well.

CHRIST IN MY LIFE

I wonder why I don't think about your Resurrection more often. Why doesn't that victory make a bigger difference in my attitudes and reactions? You rose from the dead. You showed your power over the wind and the sea, and over death itself. You are the same Lord who comes to me in Holy Communion, who waits for me patiently in the Tabernacle. Lord, increase my faith...

I know I am supposed to trust you in the midst of the storms, but Lord, it's not easy. The storms come and I often cave in. Where is my faith in those moments? You asked your apostles that question, but I ask you: why don't I believe more firmly? Why don't I trust more easily? Why, Lord, do I advance so slowly? Have mercy on me, Lord. Teach me. I trust in you, I really do...

Mary, you learned perfectly the most important lesson – the path to true happiness: to hear God's word and put it into practice. Teach me what you learned. That's all I want to do. In my work, to work as he would have me; in my family, to be patient and selfless as he would have me; in my prayer, to be humble; in my relationships, helpful, kind, and forgiving. Mary, Seat of Wisdom, make me wise...

I have little doubt that when St. George had killed the dragon he was heartily afraid of the princess.

G.K. CHESTERTON

A woman's sensibilities play a great part in the life of a family and often actually determine its course, and these same sensibilities should play their part in the life of the nation and of mankind as a whole.

POPE PIUS XII

My Mother

Who fed me from her gentle breast
And hushed me in her arms to rest,
And on my cheek sweet kisses prest?
My mother.

When sleep forsook my open eye,
Who was it sung sweet lullaby
And rocked me that I should not cry?
My mother.

Who sat and watched my infant head
When sleeping in my cradle bed,
And tears of sweet affection shed?
My mother.

When pain and sickness made me cry,
Who gazed upon my heavy eye
And wept, for fear that I should die?
My mother.

Who ran to help me when I fell
And would some pretty story tell,
Or kiss the part to make it well?
My mother.

Who taught my infant lips to pray,
To love God's holy word and day,
And walk in wisdom's pleasant way?
My mother.

And can I ever cease to be
Affectionate and kind to thee
Who wast so very kind to me,
My mother.

Oh no, the thought I cannot bear;
And if God please my life to spare
I hope I shall reward thy care,
My mother.

When thou art feeble, old and gray,
My healthy arm shall be thy stay,
And I will soothe thy pains away,
My mother.

And when I see thee hang thy head,
'Twill be my turn to watch thy bed,
And tears of sweet affection shed,
My mother.

JANE TAYLOR

The Mother's Expertise

Babies need not to be taught a trade, but to be introduced to a world. To put the matter shortly, woman is generally shut up in a house with a human being at the time when he asks all the questions that there are, and some that there aren't. It would be odd if she retained any of the narrowness of a specialist.

Now if anyone says that this duty of general enlightenment (even when freed from modern rules and hours, and exercised more spontaneously by a more protected person) is in itself too exacting and oppressive, I can understand the view. I can only answer that our race has thought it worthwhile to cast this burden on women in order to keep commonsense in the world. But when people begin to talk about this domestic duty as not merely difficult but trivial and dreary, I simply give up the question. For I cannot with the utmost energy of imagination conceive what they mean.

When domesticity, for instance, is called drudgery, all the difficulty arises from a double meaning in the word. If drudgery only means dreadfully hard work, I admit the woman drudges in the home, as a man might drudge at the Cathedral of Amiens or drudge behind a gun at Trafalgar. But if it means that the hard work is more heavy because it is trifling, colorless, and of small import to the soul, then as I say, I give it up; I do not know what the words mean.

To be Queen Elizabeth within a definite area, deciding sales, banquets, labors and holidays; to be Whiteley within a certain area, providing toys, boots, sheets cakes. and books, to be Aristotle within a certain area, teaching morals, manners, theology, and hygiene; I can understand how this might exhaust the mind, but I cannot imagine how it could narrow it. How can it be a large career to tell other people's children about the Rule of Three, and a small career to tell one's own children about the universe? How can it be broad to be the same thing to everyone, and narrow to be everything to someone? No; a woman's function is laborious, but because it is gigantic, not because it is minute, I will pity Mrs. Jones for the hugeness of her task; I will never pity her for its smallness.

G.K. CHESTERTON, *WHAT'S WRONG WITH THE WORLD*

Choosing the Better Part

*"From the top of a hill the rain flows down to
the valley. Just as more water collects at the
bottom of the hill, so Mary, sitting in a low
place at the feet of Jesus, listening to His words,
receives more than Martha, standing and
serving the temporal needs of her Master.
Mary, loving Jesus, the one thing needed,
is in port. Martha, occupying herself about
many things, is still at sea."*

St Augustine

LUKE 10:38-42

*In the course of their journey he came to a village, and
a woman named Martha welcomed him into her house. She
had a sister called Mary, who sat down at the Lord's feet and
listened to him speaking. Now Martha who was distracted
with all the serving said, 'Lord, do you not care that my sister
is leaving me to do the serving all by myself? Please tell her
to help me.' But the Lord answered: 'Martha, Martha,' he
said, 'you worry and fret about so many things, and yet few
are needed, indeed only one. It is Mary who has chosen the
better part; it is not to be taken from her.'*

CHRIST THE LORD

If Christ truly is the one Lord of life and history, the
one Savior, the one Way, Truth, and Life (and he is), then
it is certain that "only one" thing is needed for a fulfilling,
meaningful, and fruitful life: to stay as close to him as
possible at all times. When we address Christ from our

hearts as Lord, we acknowledge our conviction that he truly is our one thing necessary, and he will be as pleased with us for doing so as he was with Mary.

The Lord already is the one thing needed. Our task is to choose to shape our lives accordingly. Jesus doesn't congratulate Mary because she won the spiritual lottery or had received a particularly beautiful soul from God. He praises her because she has "chosen the better part." She chooses it. She chooses to submit to the Lord, to let him be for her what he in truth is for everyone – that one needed thing.

Once again, we are confronted with this amazing truth about Christ's Kingship: he offers the benefits of his rule to all people, but he leaves each person supremely free to accept or reject them. And the offer is not a one-time affair. Martha had chosen to busy herself with her own plans on this occasion, but you can bet she adjusted her behavior the next time the Lord came around. Mary had chosen to adore the Lord this time, but she would still be free to make the same or a different choice the next time. Each and every time we choose to give Christ and his will priority in our lives, we are pleasing him and extending the borders of his Kingdom in our lives. And every time we bring his message to others, we give them a chance to do the same.

CHRIST THE TEACHER ❧

We shouldn't berate Martha too much – she also is a saint, and she was also much loved by the Lord. But she needed to learn a lesson. She needed to learn that what we do for Christ has to flow out of what we are for him – his true and devoted friends. It is easy to overload our agenda with so many activities and commitments – good and beneficial as they may be – that we lose sight of our goal: to know, love, and imitate Christ more each day. Only that will give meaning to our lives; only that will equip us to help others find meaning; only that will fill us with the joy we long for. If we are separated from the vine, we cannot bear fruit (cf. John 15:5), but if we seek first the Kingdom, everything else will fall into place (cf. Mt 6:33).

The crucial sign that we may be following Martha's footsteps a little too closely is a waning life of prayer. When we skimp on our prayer life, on that precious time that we spend, as Mary did, "at the Lord's feet listening to him speaking," we need to stop and check our spiritual vital signs. Maybe we have allowed ourselves to become so "distracted with all the serving" that we have forgotten why we should be serving in the first place.

CHRIST THE FRIEND

Christ was glad to be served, but he was even gladder to be loved. He yearns for our love. When we come before him at the final judgment, he will be less interested in our résumé of achievements than in the love with which we achieved them. He was happy that Mary wanted to listen to him, wanted to sit beside him and spend time with him. That is why he became man in the first place – to make himself available, to offer his friendship. This desire was so strong that he invented a way to extend his real presence to all times and places through the sacrament of the Eucharist. In every tabernacle throughout the world he is available 24/7, just for us, just because he loves us.

CHRIST IN MY LIFE

I want to choose the better part every day – every moment of every day. I believe in you completely; I want to live wholly for you. Whose kingdom could I possibly prefer?

My own? Save me from that! Someone else's? But who is as wise as you, who is as powerful as you? Who is as loving as you? Thy Kingdom come, Lord, thy will be done...

I want to build your Kingdom, fulfill my apostolate, and win souls over to your friendship. I want to do so much for you! But I know that my heart is not yet completely pure. The infection of egoism is still there, albeit on the wane because of your grace. So keep me humble, Lord. Keep me focused on you and your Kingdom – not on myself and my achievements...

Thank you for staying with me in the Eucharist. Now I always have a chance to sit at your feet and listen to your words and your heartbeats. I need that. I need a real place, a real presence. Thank you, Lord. Never let me take this great gift for granted. With the love of your heart, inflame my heart...

Men are what their mothers made them.

RALPH WALDO EMERSON

Limbo

The ancient greyness shifted
Suddenly and thinned
Like mist upon the moors
Before a wind.
An old, old prophet lifted
A shining face and said:
"He will be coming soon.
The Son of God is dead;
He died this afternoon."

A murmurous excitement stirred
All souls.
They wondered if they dreamed
Save one old man who seemed
Not even to have heard.

And Moses standing,
Hushed them all to ask
If any had a welcome song prepared.
If not, would David take the task?
And if they cared
Could not the three young children sing
The Benedicite, the canticle of praise
They made when God kept them from
        perishing
In the fiery blaze?

A breath of spring surprised them,
Stilling Moses' words.
No one could speak, remembering
The first fresh flowers,

The little singing birds.
Still others thought of fields new ploughed
Or apple trees
All blossom-boughed.
Or some, the way a dried bed fills
With water
Laughing down green hills.
The fisherfolk dreamed of the foam
On bright blue seas.
The one old man who had not stirred
Remembered home.

And there He was
Splendid as the morning sun and fair
As only God is fair.
And they, confused with joy,
Knelt to adore
Seeing that He wore
Five crimson stars
He never had before.

No canticle at all was sung.
None toned a psalm, or raised a greeting song.
A silent man alone
Of all that throng
Found tongue
Not any other.

Close to His heart
When the embrace was done,
Old Joseph said,
"How is Your Mother,
How is Your Mother, Son?"

SISTER MARY ADA

Integral Complementarity

We are then told that, from the very beginning, man has been created "male and female" (Gn 1:27). Scripture itself provides the interpretation of this fact: even though man is surrounded by the innumerable creatures of the created world, he realizes that *he is alone* (cf. Gn 2:20). God intervenes in order to help him escape from this situation of solitude: "It is not good that the man should be alone; I will make him a helper fit for him" (Gn 2:18).

The creation of woman is thus marked from the outset by *the principle of help:* a help which is not one-sided but *mutual*. Woman complements man, just as man complements woman: men and women are *complementary*. Womanhood expresses the "human" as much as manhood does, but in a different and complementary way.

When the Book of Genesis speaks of "help," it is not referring merely to *acting,* but also to *being*. Womanhood and manhood are complementary *not only from the physical and psychological points of view,* but also from the *ontological*. It is only through the duality of the "masculine" and the "feminine" that the "human" finds full realization.

POPE JOHN PAUL II, *LETTER TO WOMEN*, JUNE 29, 1995, #7

The Sweet Scent of Love

*"An egg given during life for love of God is more profitable
for eternity than a cathedral full of gold given after death."*
-St Albert the Great

John 12:1-11

*Six days before the Passover, Jesus went to Bethany, where Lazarus
was, whom he had raised from the dead. They gave a dinner for him
there; Martha waited on them and Lazarus was among those at table.
Mary brought in a pound of very costly ointment, pure nard, and with
it anointed the feet of Jesus, wiping them with her hair; the house was
full of the scent of the ointment. Then Judas Iscariot – one of his disciples,
the man who was to betray him – said, 'Why wasn't this ointment sold
for three hundred denarii, and the money given to the poor?' He said this,
not because he cared about the poor, but because he was a thief; he was in
charge of the common fund and used to help himself to the contributions.
So Jesus said, 'Leave her alone; she had to keep this scent for the day
of my burial. You have the poor with you always, you will not always
have me.' Meanwhile a large number of Jews heard that he was there
and came not only on account of Jesus but also to see Lazarus whom he
had raised from the dead. Then the chief priests decided to kill Lazarus
as well, since it was on his account that many of the Jews were leaving
them and believing in Jesus.*

CHRIST THE LORD ✍

Mary's exquisite gesture of love illustrates in three
ways the utter uniqueness of Christ and the corresponding
uniqueness of our friendship with him.

First, she gives Jesus her best. The ointment was rare,
expensive, and precious. Jesus deserves our complete loyalty,
not our leftovers. We have received everything from him;

we will live forever in his company because of his mercy and love. The only appropriate response to God's generosity is complete abandonment to his goodness and unflinching obedience to his will. Mary shows that she understands this by pouring out upon him her "very costly ointment."

Second, she anoints his feet. The common way to show honor to a guest was through anointing his head. But Mary understood that she could confer no honor upon Christ; he was the Lord, he already possessed infinite dignity. Instead of bestowing honor from a position of superiority, as hosts could normally presume to do for guests who entered their own homes, she humbles herself. In an absolute sense, we cannot do favors for Christ – what does he lack that we can supply? But we can give thanks to him for the favor he has given to us – his coming among us and taking up residence in the needs of our neighbors provides us an opportunity to return love for love. Serving the Lord requires humility of heart.

Third, she wipes his feet with her hair. In Palestine at the time, women covered their hair in public. Mary defies this protocol. Her love for the Master frees her from the shackles of convention and the fears of ridicule. Christian faith is creative. The Lord always has more to give, so when we follow him sincerely, he shatters our human limitations and leads us to new horizons of generosity, new levels of fruitfulness, and new experiences of his goodness.

CHRIST THE TEACHER ❧

Jesus defends Mary's gesture on the grounds that the time for such deeds is short. This applies to every human life. Opportunities for love – for the creative, beautiful, saving deeds of self-forgetful generosity – present themselves each day. But if they are not seized, they disappear. How many times have we regretted not issuing a word of encouragement when the idea occurred to us? How many spouses, children, and friends have gazed sadly on the corpse of a loved one, desperately yearning to turn back the clock, to have just five more minutes to express the love that they had failed to show? How many chances to brighten up our neighbor's day or give glory to God in a detail of fidelity or with a brief prayer hover around us as we rush through life thinking only about ourselves? The time to love, the time to give, the time to be the noble child of God that in our hearts we know we are called to be – that time is now.

CHRIST THE FRIEND

"Martha waited on them..."

Martha: How can I describe to you that scene? Something new was in the Lord's eyes in those last days before his Passion. It was a new intensity, a new determination. Maybe "new" isn't the right word – it was just more of what had always been there, more intensity, more determination, more attention, more love. And it spread to everyone around him. I will never forget watching him at dinner, surrounded by his apostles, with Mary, so content, sitting at his feet and the other guests unable to look away from him. He was like a glowing hearth that drew in and warmed everyone around him. His presence filled everyone with light and vigor and a freshness of life.

What the aroma of Mary's perfume was for our senses, Jesus had already been for our minds and hearts. Whenever I smelled perfume after that day, it reminded me of the gentle power of his presence, which since then has never left me. And I knew that just as the perfume filled the house with its sweet and delicious scent, just so the Lord's life-giving presence was going to spread and fill every corner of history and the world.

CHRIST IN MY LIFE

Teach me to love you as I should, Lord. Turn me around – I don't want to keep gazing in the mirror and worrying about what others think of me and how I can achieve more than them. I want to gaze at you, at your truth, at the beauty of your Kingdom. I want to care only about pouring out my life in your service, like Mary's perfume, so that I can spread the fullness of life to those around me...

I wonder if I have it too easy, Lord. Maybe if my life were a bit less comfortable and pleasant I would more easily remember that I am here to fulfill a mission, not just to have a good time. You lived your life so intensely, focusing on your Father's will and the mission he had given you. And that intensity, that focus, was the source of your joy and fruitfulness. Help me, Lord, to follow your example...

Lord Jesus, you have already given me so much, but I want to ask you to come anew into my life, to make me experience again the sweet aroma of your presence. I forget so easily, Lord. The troubles of life dull my faith and hope. I need you to come and dine with me, to let me sit at your feet and drink in your wisdom. I want to keep fighting for your Kingdom. Lord Jesus, give me strength...

When it comes to
setting women free
from every kind of exploitation
and domination, the Gospel contains
an ever relevant message which goes back
to the attitude of Jesus Christ himself.
Transcending the established norms of his own culture,
Jesus treated women with openness, respect, acceptance
and tenderness. In this way he honored the dignity
which women have always possessed according
to God's plan and in his love.

POPE JOHN PAUL II

Maia's Secret

Maia Morgenstern is the Romanian actress who so brilliantly depicted the role of Mary in Mel Gibson's film *The Passion of The Christ*. She is Jewish and doesn't believe that Jesus was the Messiah. She is a mother, however, and was pregnant with her fourth child while they were filming the movie.

After the first rough cut of the film was shown to cast and crew in Rome during the post-production stage, the eclectic group of international actors and artists who had worked on the film stood around in the parking lot trying to digest what they had just seen. When you work on a movie, you don't get the full impression of it. The process is rather tedious and disconnected, like making individual pieces of a mosaic one at a time, without knowing exactly how the whole story will look when the pieces are put in place. So when everyone finally had a chance to see the whole story, from start to finish, the impact was palpable. Everyone was deeply moved.

As we stood talking in the parking, I went up to Maia. I asked her, "How did you do it? You don't believe in Jesus, you don't believe in the Gospels, but you were the perfect Mary. You showed us her love, her faith, her strength, her suffering, her hope – everything! How did you do it?" Her answer was humbling, and revelatory.

"Well," she began, "at first I tried to play each emotion individually. I tried anger, then sadness. But something was missing, so then I tried frustration, confusion, denial. But nothing worked. Righteous indignation, fear, desperation… I just couldn't get it! And then it dawned on me. I'm his mother. And that's when it clicked. *I'm his mother!* I just have to be with him. I can't let him suffer alone. And that was it."

JOHN BARTUNEK, LC, *INSIDE THE PASSION*

*If Americans can be divorced for "incompatibility
of temper," I cannot conceive why they are not all divorced.
I have known many happy marriages, but never
a compatible one. The whole aim of marriage is to
fight through and survive the instant when
incompatibility becomes unquestionable.
For a man and a woman, as such,
are incompatible.*

C.K. CHESTERTON

A Parting Gift

"Mary has truly become the Mother of all believers. Men and women of every time and place have recourse to her motherly kindness and her virginal purity and grace, in all their needs and aspirations, their joys and sorrows, their moments of loneliness and their common endeavors."

POPE BENEDICT XVI, *DEUS CARITAS EST*, 42

JOHN 19:17-30

Then they took charge of Jesus, and carrying his own cross he went out of the city to the place of the skull or, as it was called in Hebrew, Golgotha, where they crucified him with two others, one on either side with Jesus in the middle. Pilate wrote out a notice and had it fixed to the cross; it ran: 'Jesus the Nazarene, King of the Jews'. This notice was read by many of the Jews, because the place where Jesus was crucified was not far from the city, and the writing was in Hebrew, Latin and Greek. So the Jewish chief priests said to Pilate, 'You should not write King of the Jews, but This man said: I am King of the Jews'. Pilate answered, 'What I have written, I have written'. When the soldiers had finished crucifying Jesus they took his clothing and divided it into four shares, one for each soldier. His undergarment was seamless, woven in one piece from neck to hem; so they said to one another, 'Instead of tearing it, let's throw dice to decide who is to have it'. In this way the words of scripture were fulfilled: They shared out my clothing among them. They cast lots for my clothes. This is exactly what the soldiers did. Near the cross of Jesus stood his mother and his mother's sister, Mary the wife of Clopas, and Mary of Magdala. Seeing his mother and the disciple he loved standing near her, Jesus said to his mother, 'Woman, this is your son'. Then to the disciple he said, 'This is your mother'. And from that moment the disciple made a place for her in his home. After this, Jesus knew that everything had now been completed, and to fulfil the scripture perfectly he said: 'I am thirsty'. A jar-full of vinegar stood there, so putting a sponge soaked in the vinegar on a hyssop stick they held it up to his mouth. After Jesus had taken the vinegar he said, 'It is accomplished'; and bowing his head he gave up his spirit.

CHRIST THE LORD ❧

Even as Jesus' last drops of strength ebb away on the cross, he shows once again that he is the Lord of life and history. "To fulfill the scripture perfectly," St John tells us, Jesus said, "I am thirsty," and a sponge full of vinegar (the Greek word can also refer to cheap wine) was lifted up to his lips on a hyssop stick.

The flexible, willowlike wood of the hyssop plant was expressly designated for ritual purification in the Old Covenant. God had commanded his people to spread the blood of the Passover lambs on the lintels of their houses using a hyssop stick (Ex 12:22). He had commanded Israel to purify lepers and houses where leprosy has sprung up with sacrificial blood sprinkled by a hyssop stick (cf. Lv 14, Nm 19). Moses had used a hyssop stick to distribute the sacrificial blood during the ceremony that established the Old Covenant at Sinai (Heb 9:19).

Is it only a coincidence that at the time when Jesus' blood is being poured out to purify the world itself from its sin, a hyssop stick is used to hold a sponge to his parched, cracked, and bloodstained lips? If it were, St John would not have made a point of identifying the type of wood. It was no coincidence. It is yet another sign, given for our sake, to convince us that the Crucified One is exactly who he claimed to be: the Son of God, the Word of Life and Redeemer of the world who governs and orders the universe in all its grandeur and in the tiniest details. Jesus Christ is Lord; nothing escapes his rule.

CHRIST THE TEACHER

Jesus' final words were, "It is accomplished." It sums up what St John has repeated again and again throughout his Gospel: Jesus lived life focused on his mission. As his life draws to its close, he declares that that mission has been fulfilled. He had given himself completely – even to the point of sharing the very clothes on his back.

Jesus is the model for every Christian. He is also our Savior, Lord, brother, and companion, but he is still our model. And so, if he lived life focused on his mission, so should we. In this fallen world, the human family has forgotten who they are. They have come to think of themselves as autonomous mini-gods, instead of as God's stewards. In the original plan of Creation, the human family had been given the task of cultivating and protecting the Garden of Eden. We were created "to live in communion with God, in whom we find our happiness," as the Catechism reminds us (45). But that communion was never meant to be something passive. It is a relationship in which we glorify God through discovering his goodness in prayer and in action – as we do the work we were created to do, we become the saints we were created to be.

Jesus restores the possibility of that communion through reversing Adam's rebellious disobedience. He also points the way for us to partake of that restoration: by learning once again to see our lives as a mission. In this epoch of

Redemption, the mission is not merely to cultivate and protect the garden, but to build the Kingdom of Christ, which we do the same way Jesus established it, seeking and fulfilling God's will: "I seek to do not my own will but the will of him who sent me" (Jn 5:30).

CHRIST THE FRIEND

The beloved disciple mentioned in this passage is commonly considered to be the author himself, St John. Only he records Jesus' final will and testament, in which Jesus places his mother Mary under John's care and John under hers. St John was writing his Gospel later in life, when he was already an old man. For him to emphasize this detail means that it was significant not only for him personally, but for the whole Church. And indeed the Church has always considered this gesture of Jesus to be much more than a practical arrangement.

Jesus is on the verge of completing his earthly mission. As he does so, the mission of the Church (represented in a special way by the "beloved disciple," because the Church is Jesus' beloved) is just beginning. By explicitly transferring the care of the Church (the beloved disciple) to Mary's motherly attention and entrusting Mary to John in a filial way, Jesus extends Mary's mission. She had been the Mother of Christ, the head of the Church, and now she is to be the Mother of the whole body, the members of the Church. Christ had only one thing left to give as he breathed his last breath – his own Mother, and he didn't grudge us even that. Each follower of Christ, to enter fully into God's family and to have Christ as a true brother, has to follow John's example: "And from that moment the disciple made a place for her in his home."

Mary: I didn't choose to become Jesus' mother; that was God's choice. How could I have ever chosen for myself such an exalted role, when I always knew that I was only a blade of grass in the foothills beneath the mountain of God? Only God in his wisdom and goodness can give one of his creatures such a sublime mission. And though I didn't choose it, how much joy it gave me! Even the sorrow of his pain on Calvary filled me with a certain spiritual joy, because it allowed me to suffer too; it showed him in a new way that I would never leave him or doubt him. And I didn't choose to become your Mother either; that too was his choice. How could I have presumed to take upon myself such an exalted task, to be mother to a child born of water and the Holy Spirit? Only God in his goodness could give me such a joyful and worthy mission. And now I watch over you just as I watched over him; I accompany you just as I accompanied him; I love you just as I loved him. He made me Queen of Heaven so that I could be your refuge and solace.

CHRIST IN MY LIFE

Nothing escapes your rule. Down to the tiny detail of a hyssop stick on Calvary, you govern every speck of the cosmos and every wrinkle of human history. You are the Lord. You are my Lord. Increase my faith, Lord. I want to rejoice in the peace of knowing you more deeply and trusting you more unconditionally...

For so many people, life is only a mystery, Lord. They don't know that it is a mission. They seek to refresh their souls at empty wells. Teach them about your Kingdom! Call out to them so that they stop spiraling further down into sterile self-absorption! In you, Lord, life takes on the dimension of adventure that we all know it should take on. Ring out your message, Lord, louder and clearer...

Mary, how do you guide me? I don't see your face or hear your voice. But I know you are faithful to God's will, and it is his will for you to teach and nourish me as my mother in grace. How do you do it? You instruct me by your example: you stood at the foot of the cross, firm and faithful because your love was true and total. Teach me how to embrace fully the will of God, even when it means embracing the cross...

Somebody's Mother

The woman was old and ragged and gray
And bent with the chill of the Winter's day.

The street was wet with a recent snow
And the woman's feet were aged and slow.

She stood at the crossing and waited long,
Alone, uncared for, amid the throng

Of human beings who passed her by
Nor heeded the glance of her anxious eye.

Down the street, with laughter and shout,
Glad in the freedom of "school let out,"

Came the boys like a flock of sheep,
Hailing the snow piled white and deep.

Past the woman so old and gray
Hastened the children on their way.

Nor offered a helping hand to her
So meek, so timid, afraid to stir

Lest the carriage wheels or the horses' feet
Should crowd her down in the slippery street.

At last came one of the merry troop,
The gayest laddie of all the group;

He paused beside her and whispered low,
"I'll help you cross, if you wish to go."

Her aged hand on his strong young arm
She placed, and so, without hurt or harm,

He guided the trembling feet along,
Proud that his own were firm and strong.

Then back again to his friends he went,
His young heart happy and well content.

"She's somebody's mother, boys, you know,
For all she's aged and poor and slow,

"And I hope some fellow will lend a hand
To help my mother, you understand,

"If ever she's poor and old and gray,
When her own dear boy is far away."

And "somebody's mother" bowed low her head
In her home that night, and the prayer she said

Was, "God be kind to the noble boy,
Who is somebody's son, and pride and joy!"

MARY DOW BRINE

The Genius of Women

Necessary emphasis should be placed on the *"genius of women,"* not only by considering great and famous women of the past or present, but also those *ordinary* women who reveal the gift of their womanhood by placing themselves at the service of others in their everyday lives. For in giving themselves to others each day women fulfill their deepest vocation. Perhaps more than men, women *acknowledge the person,* because they see persons with their hearts. They see them independently of various ideological or political systems. They see others in their greatness and limitations; they try to go out to them and *help them.* In this way the basic plan of the Creator takes flesh in the history of humanity and there is constantly revealed, in the variety of vocations, that *beauty* – not merely physical, but above all spiritual – which God bestowed from the very beginning on all, and in a particular way on women…

The moral and spiritual strength of a woman is joined to her awareness that *God entrusts the human being to her in a special way.* Of course, God entrusts every human being to each and every other human being. But this entrusting concerns women in a special way – precisely by reason of their femininity – and this in a particular way determines their vocation…

A woman is strong because of her awareness of this entrusting, strong because of the fact that God "entrusts the human being to her," always and in every way, even in the situations of social discrimination in which she may find herself. This awareness and this fundamental vocation speak to women of the dignity which they receive from God himself, and this makes them "strong" and strengthens their vocation.

POPE JOHN PAUL II, *MULIERIS DIGNITATEM,* 12,30

Love and Life

"You are alive! Your murderers handled your life like farmers: they sowed it like grain deep in the earth, for it to spring up and raise with itself a multitude of men."

St Ephraem

LUKE 24:1-12

On the first day of the week, at the first sign of dawn, they went to the tomb with the spices they had prepared. They found that the stone had been rolled away from the tomb, but on entering discovered that the body of the Lord Jesus was not there. As they stood there not knowing what to think, two men in brilliant clothes suddenly appeared at their side. Terrified, the women lowered their eyes. But the two men said to them, 'Why look among the dead for someone who is alive? He is not here; he has risen. Remember what he told you when he was still in Galilee: that the Son of Man had to be handed over into the power of sinful men and be crucified, and rise again on the third day?' And they remembered his words. When the women returned from the tomb they told all this to the Eleven and to all the others. The women were Mary of Magdala, Joanna, and Mary the mother of James. The other women with them also told the apostles, but this story of theirs seemed pure nonsense, and they did not believe them. Peter, however, went running to the tomb. He bent down and saw the binding cloths but nothing else; he then went back home, amazed at what had happened.

CHRIST THE LORD ❧

No one escapes death. Emperors die, geniuses die, business tycoons die – death is the great equalizer, the great reminder that we are not gods. But Christ rose from the dead; he conquered the grave. He died, yet he is still alive. He lives and reigns now, in this very moment. He is as alive as anyone walking the earth today, even though he truly died. No other historical figure has even made such a claim, let alone given proof, century after century (through the otherwise inexplicable vitality of the Church), to substantiate the claim. The Resurrection is Christ's trump card, Christian life's unshakable foundation. This is our Lord, the definitive conqueror of sin and death. We, like Peter, should be "amazed." If we are not, we don't really know our Lord.

CHRIST THE TEACHER ❧

The Resurrection validates all of Christ's other lessons. Without it, they would be nice pieces of advice, beautiful ones even, but ultimately impractical. If his doctrine doesn't lead to true life, why make the sacrifices necessary to follow it? By rising from the dead, he confirms that his doctrine does lead to life. The Resurrection is his "most marvelous work," as St Augustine put it. The odd thing is that he entrusts the announcement of this all-important message to his weak and fragile followers. Unless we spread the news, it won't get spread at all.

The news of this most marvelous work doesn't come from his own lips. He entrusts the message first to the angels, then to the women who came to his tomb. Only after the women hear the news from the angels does he appear to them (cf. St Matthew's version); and only after the women have announced the news to the Apostles does he appear to them. This is the pattern of evangelization in all times and places: a personal, life-changing encounter with the living Lord is always mediated by Christian witness. We who have met the risen Jesus through the gift of faith have to announce the good news to those who have not. As St Paul put it: "But how can they call on him in whom they have not believed? And how can they believe in him of whom they have not heard? And how can they hear without someone to preach?" (Rom 10:14)

CHRIST THE FRIEND

Joanna: When the angels spoke to us, they called Jesus "someone who is alive." The words struck me, though I only had time to reflect on them later. At the time, we were so exhausted by our sadness and shocked by the bright angels and the open tomb that we couldn't think at all. I am sure we were quite incoherent when we went to tell the apostles. How beautiful are the angel's words! Jesus truly is the one most alive, because he is the one who loves the most. The cross was the testament to his immense love; the Resurrection is the testament to his overflowing life. God is love, and God is also the source of all life. True life and true love are inextricably intertwined. When Jesus offered me his friendship, he was inviting me to share in his life. That meant experiencing his love so that I could learn to love as he does, which is the path to the indescribable life he wishes to give us.

Jesus: I want my life to be your life. Imagine an iron rod being thrust into a blazing fire. Just as the cold, hard rod becomes red-hot and supple, taking on the characteristics of the fire, so your life, united in friendship to mine, will take on the intensity of my life. I came for this, that you might have life and have it in all its abundance.

CHRIST IN MY LIFE

How little I think about your Resurrection, Lord! And yet, you really did rise from the dead. Only you have done it.

I believe in your goodness, and I believe in your power. And so I will continue to seek your will for my life, because your will is both your goodness and your power custom-fitted to the needs and yearnings of my soul. Teach me to do your will...

Sometimes I am intimidated by the commission you have given me to spread your Kingdom. But you don't ask me to convert the world, you just ask me to bear witness right here and right now, with my life, and when necessary with words, to all that you have done for me. All I need to do is make myself available, and you will take care of the rest. Jesus, I trust in you...

Mary, your heart still beats with Christ's. I want to burn with the love that consumes your heart. I want to live the life of overflowing abundance, unlimited surrender, and uncontainable joy that Jesus gave to you and gives to all his saints, to everyone who trusts in him unconditionally. Let it be done to me according to his word...

A good man's work is effected by doing what he does, a woman's by being what she is.

G.K. CHESTERTON

A Mother's Love

There are times when only a Mother's love
Can understand our tears,
Can soothe our disappoints
And calm all of our fears.

There are times when only a Mother's love
Can share the joy we feel
When something we've dreamed about
Quite suddenly is real.

There are times when only a Mother's faith
Can help us on life's way
And inspire in us the confidence
We need from day to day.

For a Mother's heart and a Mother's faith
And a Mother's steadfast love
Were fashioned by the Angels
And sent from God above...

AUTHOR UNKNOWN

An email from Uncle Eddy about St Matilda
(Feast Day, March 14, entered heaven on that day in 968)

Dear Regina,

It must be a relief to have finally decided on a major. Frankly, I am quite pleased with your decision; if there's one place in academia that needs a Catholic presence, it's Women's Studies. You will do a great service to the department (and your fellow students) if you are able to combine modern scholarship and the ancient wisdom of the Church as you tackle this exciting subject. I only have one caveat for you: watch out for the anti-feminists (sometimes they conceal their true agenda by calling themselves "feminists"). They are the ones who think that true feminism consists in de-feminization, in obliterating any gender distinction except purely biological functionality. This, as you know, is contrary to human experience, as well as opposed to God's revelation. The Church has always taught and strived to live (not always successfully) a vision of gender identity based on integral complementarity: God created the human person in his image, "male and female he created them." In other words, men and women have the same human dignity, but offer complementary emotional, spiritual, biological, and intellectual traits, and only by consciously bringing these traits together will we fulfill our human vocation. True feminism, therefore, will strive to understand and release authentic femininity (and authentic masculinity) for the benefit of all and the glory of God.

I have always been impressed by the great female saints of the Church. They reveal the feminine genius in the most varied and unlikely situations, and yet (in my opinion) they are too little known. Today's saint is a perfect example. When we study medieval history we all hear about Otto the Great and how he "saved the papacy" from the Roman mob and set in motion Europe's recovery from the second wave of barbarian invasions. We almost always hear about St Bruno and his brilliant revitalization of the Church in Germany and France. We hear more than enough about the great French kings who furthered the cause of Christ in myriad ways. But have you every seen St Matilda mentioned in your textbooks?

She was Otto the Great's mother, St Bruno's mother, and her daughters married into the great French families, infusing fresh devotion where it had dangerously waned. She was the daughter of nobles and grew up under the care of her grandmother in a German convent. There she grew to womanhood and exceeded all her peers, so the records say, in beauty, piety, and learning.

She married the German king's son (who was eventually made emperor) and devoted all her energy and talent to keeping a royal house worthy of being called Christian. Towards her servants and the members of her court she acted less like a queen and more like a loving mother, and they repaid her with diehard loyalty and confidence. She made her marriage to Henry a happy one for the whole family, and never failed to balance out his tendencies to superficiality and impulsiveness. As a result, his rule was marked by success and prosperity in every way (the people always attributed his victories in war more to her prayers than to his prowess).

As a mother, she suffered much at her five children's squabbles and excesses, but the results of her efforts speak for themselves. As long as she lived the wealth and influence of the imperial court was ever at the service of the Church, of the poor, and of the sick. After her husband died, she dedicated herself even more intensely to caring for the poor, and to her many monastic and conventual foundations. Her last days were spent visiting these religious houses, and she passed away in one of them. She was buried beside her husband, and from the moment of her death the crowds hailed and venerated her as a saint.

The influence of that one woman reverberated down through the centuries. Some would argue that it was felt even up to the French Revolution. She had indeed released in her own heart and life the feminine genius, and it flowed out from her in a way proper to her times and circumstances. May your studies help you tap into the same genius, so that it can have a similar influence in these very different times and circumstances.

Sincerely,

your uncle, Eddy

Taking the Jesus Risk

*"Our Lord was trodden underfoot by death, and
in turn trod upon death as upon a road."*

ST EPHRAEM

JOHN 20:11-18

*Meanwhile Mary stayed outside near the tomb, weeping.
Then, still weeping, she stooped to look inside, and saw two
angels in white sitting where the body of Jesus had been, one
at the head, the other at the feet. They said, 'Woman, why are
you weeping?' 'They have taken my Lord away' she replied
'and I don't know where they have put him.' As she said this
she turned round and saw Jesus standing there, though she
did not recognise him. Jesus said, 'Woman, why are you
weeping? Who are you looking for?' Supposing him to be the
gardener, she said, 'Sir, if you have taken him away, tell me
where you have put him, and I will go and remove him'. Jesus
said, 'Mary!' She knew him then and said to him in Hebrew,
'Rabbuni!' – which means Master. Jesus said to her, 'Do not
cling to me, because I have not yet ascended to the Father.
But go and find the brothers, and tell them: I am ascending
to my Father and your Father, to my God and your God.' So
Mary of Magdala went and told the disciples that she had
seen the Lord and that he had said these things to her.*

CHRIST THE LORD

The first time Jesus speaks in the Gospel of John, he
asks Peter and John a question: "What do you want?" In the
Greek, his question to Mary Magdalene on the morning of
his resurrection (here translated "Who are you looking for?")
uses the same verb and the same pronoun. Only the case of

the pronoun is different, turning the "what" of Chapter 1 into the "who" of Chapter 20. The verb has multiple shades of meaning, but most translations use "look for" or "seek" in both instances. The distinction between "want" and "seek" is subtle; you would never seek something that you don't want, and if you really do want something, you will naturally seek it out.

And so Jesus' question to Mary Magdalene, though he asks it after his Resurrection, brings us full circle, back to the beginning of the story. He asked the same question of his first followers as he did of Mary after the Resurrection: "What do you want? Who are you looking for?" It shows that Jesus always cares about the same thing – the state of our hearts. In the depth of our souls we decide the direction of our lives by deciding what we are going to look for. And this is what matters to Jesus. He is the Lord, the King, but he doesn't rule governments or boards of trustees – he rules hearts (and those in turn rule governments and boards of trustees). He asks us each day, in the inner sanctuary of our consciences, what we are looking for, what we desire, and what we want. If we truly want the fullness of life that he came to bring us, he will be able to give it to us, because we will be willing to take the risk of leaving behind the comfort of self-centeredness to launch out on the adventure of self-giving.

On the first Easter morning, Mary Magdalene might have thought that the risk she had taken wasn't panning out, but then the Lord appeared and ended her search. Trusting in Jesus Christ the Lord is a risk that always pans out.

CHRIST THE TEACHER

Christ rose so that we too may someday rise. He conquered death so that we could look forward to everlasting life in the intense and indescribable excitement of heavenly fulfillment. In his post-resurrection appearances, he gives us clues about what that fullness of life will be like. One thing we notice right away is that his resurrected body, though a real body (St John will tell us later that the apostles can see and touch the wounds in his hands and side), has been somehow transformed. Mary Magdalene doesn't recognize him at first. He seems to appear and disappear at will and even pass through walls and doors.

Theologians call the resurrected body a "glorified body." A popular but mistaken idea among many Christians is that life in heaven is purely spiritual. After the last judgment, however, when we all have been raised ("Those who did good will rise again to life; and those who did evil, to condemnation" Jn 5:29), those who are welcomed into heaven will receive the fullness of life, which, for human beings, includes bodily existence. Just as Jesus and Mary are right now, at this very moment, physically present in heaven, so we will enjoy everlasting life not only with our souls but with glorified bodies. Much theological speculation has gone into describing the characteristics of our glorified state, but suffice it to say that it will be exempt from the physical sufferings and limitations of life on earth and will far surpass – very far – the physical delights of life on earth. It is something we should look forward to, something we should hope for, because it is something God wishes to give us.

CHRIST THE FRIEND

Before Mary Magdalene was searching for Jesus, he was already watching over her. He lets her search, sorrowing, only so that the joy of their reunion will be that much more intense. It seems, in fact, that he wants to give her a chance to believe in the Resurrection before experiencing it. And so, the angels announce to her the Good News. But neither the daunting presence of the angels nor their remarkable announcement satisfied Mary. For her, nothing but the Lord himself, his very presence, would do. She turns away from them, because they can't give her that presence. But she perseveres in her search – asking the gardener for what the angels couldn't give. This perseverance moves the heart of Christ, and the first recorded appearance of the Resurrected Lord ensues.

Jesus came to earth in search of our love. So if we truly love him, and if we show it by seeking him in spite of obstacles and failures, how can he resist rewarding our desire? To experience the revolution of Christ in our lives, it is enough to want to do so – and to keep on wanting to.

Jesus: My child, while you are searching for me, I am already at your side. I never abandon you. Where can you hide from my love? Where can you flee from my presence? If you rise up on the wings of the dawn and set down across the farthest sea, my hand will still be guiding you, my strong arms will still be holding you fast. All that your heart seeks you will find in me. But you have to keep looking, because you're not ready to receive everything right away. If only you knew how much I long to fill every moment of your life with the light and warmth of my divine heart! I am always knocking at the door of your heart – my knocks give rise to your weeping and searching, just as they did with my faithful friend Mary Magdalene...

CHRIST IN MY LIFE

What I am looking for? What do I want? You know, Lord. I want to follow you. I believe in you. My faith is puny and impure, but it's there. A myriad of other wants and desires swarm around my heart, and sometimes I let them get the upper hand, but even so, Lord, without you in my life, what direction, what hope could I possibly have? Keep me faithful to your will; never let me be separated from you...

Lord, increase my hope! You have revealed to me the truth about my final destiny. You have gone to prepare me a place in heaven. You want me to spend eternity in your company and in the company of all the saints. There the fullness of life that I have always longed for and have begun to taste here on earth will surpass my greatest longings. Lord, make these truths come to life for me...

Why do you let me weep and search? Why don't you show yourself to me always? Your ways are beyond me, Lord. But I know that they are wise. You are Wisdom and Goodness and Power and Love. It is enough for me to know you, to believe in you. That is already a gift far beyond what I deserve! O Lord, open my eyes to see your hand at work in all things, and strengthen my will to follow you more closely...